Collins

need to know?

Latin Dancing

Lyndon Wainwright
with Lynda King

Collins

First published in 2006 by Collins
an imprint of
HarperCollins Publishers
77-85 Fulham Palace Road
London W6 8JB

www.collins.co.uk

Collins is a registered trademark of HarperCollins Publishers Limited

10 09 08 07 06
6 5 4 3 2 1

A catalogue record for this book is available from the British Library

Created by: m&n publishing
Editor: Nina Sharman
Designer: Martin Hendry
Photographer: Christopher H. D. Davis
Illustrator: Lee Woodgate
Dance consultant: Lynda King
Series design: Mark Thomson
Front cover photograph: © Bananastock Ltd.
Back cover photographs: Christopher H. D. Davis

Based on material from *Let's Dance* by Lyndon Wainwright

ISBN-13: 978-0-00-723022-8
ISBN-10: 0-00-723022-2

Colour reproduction by Colourscan, Singapore
Printed and bound by Printing Express Ltd, Hong Kong

Contents

Ross

Introduction

Latin dances are all things to all men and women. They are for all ages, the young at heart as well as the young. Within the category there is an enormous variety, encompassing dances of romance, dances for the sophisticated, energetic dances, and, most importantly, dances for the social dancer. They range from the vibrant Samba of Brazil to the sinuous Rumba from Cuba, from the lively Merengue of Haiti and the Dominican Republic to the cheeky Cha Cha Cha, born in Cuba, and, to add spice to them all, the extremely popular Cuban/American Salsa.

One dance you might expect to be included in a book on Latin dance is the Tango, but because the dancing establishment categorised it as a 'ballroom' dance many years ago, it is not included here. However, Latin dances can be danced solo, and, as Disco is a solo dance, which is commonly danced to Latin rhythms, it is featured here.

The figures explained in this book will provide you with a sound foundation to enable you to enjoy the dances, and upon which you can build in order to expand your repertoire if you choose to do so. However, the joy of dancing is not the range of figures that you are able to use in each dance, but the fundamental movement in harmony with the music. It is a natural response that millions enjoy without concerning themselves as to why they like the dancing experience.

It is a pastime that the two sexes enjoy together. Each has his or her part to play, and they are different though complementary. While it is a self-evident truth that many romances start on the dance floor, dance is enjoyable in itself. This applies especially to the Latin dances where the response to the various music forms touches instinctive emotions, if not to say passions. Let the Latin dances transport you to a world without care that is good for you both mentally and physically.

Lyndon Wainwright and his partner Deirdre Baker (opposite) in a performance of the Rumba.

1 Preparing to dance

Learning to dance is not only an excellent physical activity, it also improves posture and keeps you mentally alert. Above all, it is fantastic fun – so get ready to dance. It is music that determines the style of dance and beginners should learn to listen for the all-important rhythm. Advice on music for Latin dancing is given here, together with information on what to wear. The main holds and positions used in Latin dance are explained, as well as how to use this book.

The origins of Latin dance

Originating in Cuba, Brazil, the Dominican Republic, Haiti, Columbia and other South American states, Latin-American dances are now performed in ballrooms throughout the world.

did you know?

- **Samba**
1930s: became popular in the USA and UK
- **Rumba**
1930s: introduced in the USA, then in UK
- **Cha Cha Cha**
1950s: introduced in the USA and UK
- **Salsa**
1960s: first Salsa musical recordings
mid-1970s: name and dance established in USA and UK
- **Merengue**
1950s: first heard, but not popular in the USA until the 1970s
1980s: became popular in the UK
- **Disco**
1948: first discotheque opened in Paris
1960s: established in the USA and UK

Many Latin dances, if not all, have been influenced by American popular music, creating a variety of dance forms. These Latin dances were only introduced into Western society in the 20th century and have diverse but similar origins.

The dances of every country are a conglomeration of the historical form of the dance that has been constantly amended by the dancers of each generation. Elements from the past, even many hundreds of years ago, can be found in every dance.

All Latin-American dances are influenced by the music and dances of the African slaves who were imported into the South American mainland and islands. They brought with them sophisticated music, especially rhythms and dance forms, which then became merged with those of the emigrant colonizers from Europe. For example, in Cuba, the Contradance (the French name for English Country Dance) became the Contradanza Habanera, with the adoption of a syncopated rhythm. As the dance evolved, its name became abbreviated to Danson. Some dances merely became modified, other new dances grew out of traditional forms.

The traditional Rumba developed and changed with time, and from it the Cha Cha Cha evolved. This process continued. The Cuban rhythms and a fusion of dances, Rumba, Cha Cha Cha and Mambo (among

Carole Lombard and George Raft dancing in the 1935 film, *Rumba*. Hollywood played its part in making the Rumba one of the most popular Latin American dances.

others) interacted with American rock music, and a new dance, Salsa, was the result.

In the 21st century, Latin-American dances have come much more to the fore. In addition to the Rumba, Samba and Salsa, dances such as the Lambada, Merengue, Macarena and Mambo can be seen in international dance competitions and on the dance floor.

And what of the future? There is every possibility that other Latin dances will, with time, become popular in the Western world. The Cumbia of Columbia, with its very catchy music, is certainly a possibility, as is the Corrido of Mexico and Venezuela, and the Tumba of Curacao and Aruba.

Latin dance music

Music determines what particular Latin dance you are going to perform. Each dance has its own distinctive music and you need to learn how much music is required for each step.

must know

Recommended music
- **Samba**
'Iko Iko'
'Give It Up'
'Chica Boom'
- **Rumba**
'Can You Feel The Love Tonight?'
'Frenesi'
'No Matter What'
- **Cha Cha Cha**
'Tea For Two Cha Cha'
'Pata Pata'
'Sex Bomb'
- **Salsa**
'She Knows That She Wants To'
'Esa Chica Es Mia'
'El O Yo'
- **Merengue**
'Su Mirada (Loco Loco)'
'Te La Compro'
'Soul Limbo'
- **Disco**
Disco can be danced to a wide range of readily available popular music.

We are accustomed to thinking of dancing as being something performed to music, but at its most elementary any rhythmic beat will suffice. The ticking of a metronome could do as a basis for dance steps. Of course, while the metronome does give a rhythm, it lacks any variety and expression. The rhythm section of an orchestra produces a great variety of moods and expression. The melody complements the rhythms giving more depth and colour to any musical piece.

From the point of view of the beginner it is the rhythm that is all important and for which he or she must listen. All the dances in this book are in 4/4 or 2/4 time.

This is all you need to worry about at this stage. However, for any more musically literate of you, we should mention that sometimes the second and fourth beats in a bar are more heavily accented than the first and third. Latin dances sometimes have very complex and intricate variations to the basic rhythm. Nevertheless, the basic rhythm is not lost and the complications of the Cuban influence need not worry you.

Any music can be given a Latin beat, even a nursery rhyme. In the first of these four bars of music, each 'twinkle' takes two musical crotchets that is two counts. In bar two 'little' takes two counts and 'star' (clearly longer) also lasts for two counts.

Dress to dance

The main thing to bear in mind is comfort when choosing what to wear, whether it be for practise or for social dancing. Clothing should also be flattering and appropriate for the Latin style.

Clothing should not be too restricting, especially around the legs – this is particularly true for women. It is important for many Latin dances that you are able to move the arms, legs and hips freely. Learning Latin dances that require swaying hips, such as the Rumba or the Samba with its characteristic bounce, is difficult enough but in tight clothing it will prove tricky and you will not create the right mood.

Shoes are of vital importance. They should be lightweight and with a flexible sole, if possible a leather sole. Good dancers use shoes with special 'non-skid' soles made of chrome leather or similar, but at the beginner level this is not necessary. However, the sole of the shoes should not impede movement of the foot across the floor in steps where you stroke the floor with the feet. Ladies should wear a shoe with a heel. Men should wear good-quality dress shoes, but trainers for both men and women are fine for practice sessions.

Today, women's clothing is readily available in lightweight, stretch fabric, which is ideal for dancewear.

Wearing accessories, such as this choker, can give your outfit a touch of elegance.

Dance holds and positions

Before starting to dance you will need to learn the correct holds. Couples should stand up straight with long spines. Generally, for Latin dancing, the Open Hold is adopted.

Open Hold

Stand about 15–20 cm (6–8 in) away from each other. The man holds the lady with his right hand on her back just below her left shoulder blade and with the heel of his hand almost on the side

The Open Hold is the classic one used for most Latin dancing.

The Close Hold is the stance adopted for the Merengue.

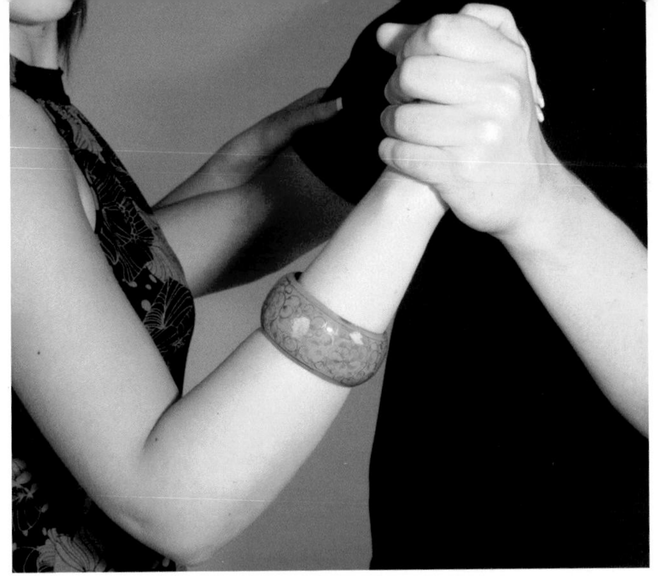

Dancers demonstrate the positioning of hands for Latin dances, such as the Rumba.

of the lady's body. He holds her right hand loosely in his left hand at a little below shoulder level or lower. The lady will rest her left hand on the upper part of the man's right arm. The main thing is to find a hold around this description that you find comfortable. As in all dances where body contact is not the norm, there will be occasions where the man will release hold of his partner with either his left or right hand. When this occurs, it will be described in the text.

A dancer demonstrates the Latin cross, which is used in the Rumba and Cha Cha Cha.

Close Hold

This is a body contact hold used in some Latin dances, especially in club dances such as the Merengue.

Both the man and lady should stand up well, with the lady's right hip positioned roughly midway between the man's hips. The man holds the lady with his right hand placed well round her back. The lady rests her left hand on the man's upper right arm just below or on his shoulder. The man holds the lady's right hand in his left hand. Good dancers may hold the hands fairly high but to start with, the man's left hand should be about level with his chin and neck. According to your relative sizes, the hold can be adjusted but the man needs to hold the lady firmly without overdoing the pressure.

How to use this book

Popular Latin dances are introduced with the assumption that readers are novices. The figures (or the routines) in each dance have been chosen to get you dancing as soon as possible.

must know

Steps and figures
A step is the movement of a foot from one position to its next position, while a group of steps is known as a figure. Each dance, for instance, Samba or Rumba, comprises several individual figures that can be joined together to form a routine. In each dance suggestions are given for ways of grouping figures.

Many of the dances in this book show simplified versions of more sophisticated figures in the hope that the experience and joy of dancing and moving to music will encourage you to delve more deeply. A visit to a local school of dance will broaden your horizons immensely. As with all disciplines, a jargon has grown up around dance analysis and here it is used only if it provides a useful shortcut to learning. All dance parlance is explained in the Glossary on page 182.

Although it is not essential, all figures start on the man's left and the lady's right foot. This helps overcome some of the uncertainty beginners have at the start of a dance.

In each figure, foot diagrams of the steps are included as an aid to following the instructions (see opposite). While these are as accurate as possible, in some cases it has been necessary to exaggerate the size of the steps in order to avoid having too many on the same point.

Most Latin dances fall into the category of non-moving dances, unlike the moving dances in Ballroom, such as the Waltz or Quickstep. In non-moving dances, all steps at beginner level are taken on the ball of the foot with the heel settling to the floor immediately after the foot is in position. The hips settle to the left and right according to the steps, and the amount of pressure placed into the floor on the supporting foot is essential in achieving this.

This is the name of the figure. Dances comprise of individual, figures that are joined together, sometimes one after another, or in a particular grouping.

On the foot diagrams, start positions for the man and the lady are given for all figures. Note that the pale foot is the left and the dark foot the right.

The length of some steps has been slightly exaggerated so that it is clear where each foot has to move to.

4 | Cha Cha Cha

The Fan

In the Fan, the man releases hold of the lady with his right hand, guides her to move to his left side and turn, so that she is facing him at roughly right angles.

must know

At the end of this figure you will end up in what dancers call the Fan position. The Fan is usually followed by the Hockey Stick (see pages 94–9).

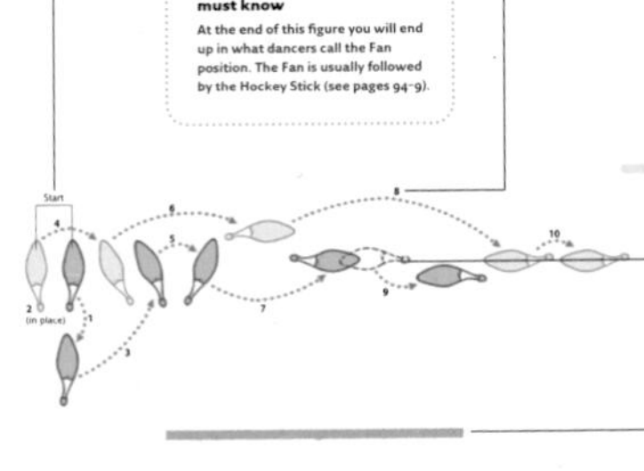

When you see a dotted foot, it means that you move your foot slightly after you have taken the main step.

A bold solid line denotes the wall. This will help you to know where to start.

count		Man's Steps
step	1	**Left foot** takes a small step forwards.
step	2	**Right foot** remains in place with the weight back onto it.
cha	3	**Left foot** takes a step to the side, turning to the left.
cha	4	**Right foot** closes towards but not up to left foot.
chah	5	**Left foot** takes a step to the side, turning to the left and lowering your left arm.
step	6	**Right foot** takes a step backwards, leading partner to step to the left of your feet, that is, 'outside partner'.
step	7	**Left foot** remains in place with the weight taken forwards onto it. Turn the lady to her left by pulling your left hand back and releasing hold of her with your right hand.
cha	8	**Right foot** takes a step to the side, turning to your left. The lady should almost be at right angles to you and stepping back away from you.
cha	9	**Left foot** closes towards right foot, still turning to your left.
chah	10	**Right foot** takes a small step to the side. You are now at right angles to your partner, holding her right hand in your left hand.

88 | need to know? Latin Dancing

count		Lady's Steps
step	1	**Right foot** takes a small step backwards.
step	2	**Left foot** remains in place with the weight forwards onto it.
cha	3	**Right foot** takes a step to the side turning to the left.
cha	4	**Left foot** closes towards but not up to right foot.
chah	5	**Right foot** takes a step to the side, turning to the right and lowering your right arm.
step	6	**Left foot** takes a step forwards to your right of both your partner's feet, that is, 'outside partner'.
step	7	**Right foot** takes a step forwards, then turn to the left on both feet to finish with your right foot backwards.
cha	8	**Left foot** takes a step backwards, still turning to the left to finish at almost right angles to your partner.
cha	9	**Right foot** closes towards left foot, still turning to the left. At this point you can cross the right foot in front of the left foot.
chah	10	**Left foot** takes a small step backwards. You are now at right angles to your partner, he is holding your right hand in his left hand.

The Fan | 89

If you learn the musical count, it will help you to maintain a good rhythm when dancing.

By reading the step-by-step instructions in conjunction with the diagrams, you will be able to practise the movements of each figure without a partner.

In Place Basic Cha Cha Chas

1
Count: step

M Left foot closes to right foot.

L Right foot closes to left foot.

2
Count: step

M Right foot marks time in place.

L Left foot marks time in place.

The step-by-step photographs generally show the position you and your partner will be in at the end of each instruction.

3
Count: cha

M Left foot to the side, starting the cha cha cha rhythm break leftwards.

L Right foot to the side, starting the cha cha cha rhythm break rightwards.

4
Count: cha

M Right foot closes towards but not up to left foot.

L Left foot closes towards but not up to right foot.

The man's and lady's instructions here are slightly abridged versions of those that accompany the foot diagrams. They read from left to right.

In Place Basic Cha Cha Chas | 85

2 Samba

This is a dance for the young at heart but not necessarily young in age. It is joyful and colourful and, while it is a fairly brisk dance, it is also intrinsically simple. The rhythmic patterns of the music, full of syncopation as we expect from all Latin dances, are easy for the beginner to hear and express. It is the dance of carnival and should be approached with that mental attitude. Leave your inhibitions behind and Samba your cares away.

A national dance

The Samba is Brazil's national dance. As is so often the case, the term is a generic one encompassing a wide range of dances that are closely related and share the same historical background.

In 1500, the Spaniard, Vincente Yánez Pinzon, became the first European to land in Brazil. Four months later, the country was claimed for Portugal by Pedro Alvarez Cabral who established the first settlement at Salvador de Bahia. What has this to do with a popular dance form? The reason is that national dances are often a microcosm of a country's history, and this is never so apparent than with Brazil and its national dance, the Samba.

did you know?

Fados and folias

To the melting pot of dance came the music and dance culture of Portugal. Of particular interest are fados and folias. Fado means fate, and this guitar-based music has a wistful character. Folias are expressive dance forms, which feature striking, large, extravagant head-dresses for the women. Perhaps this could be the foundation for the highly elaborate creations worn by the women in the annual Rio carnival.

Cultural mix

Following the appropriation of the country, many Portuguese people moved to Brazil and brought with them the music and dance forms of their native country. A consequence of the annexation of South American countries was the deplorable importation of slaves from Africa. This resulted in the country becoming a mix of three cultures. The native Brazilian Indians had long-established religions, many of a voodoo nature, such as Macumba and its religious dance ceremonies and music. However, the native Indians were treated very badly by the invaders, and little of their culture has had a major impact upon the development of today's dance forms.

Out of Africa

The greatest influence on the music and dance of Brazil came from the slaves who brought with them their traditional music and dance forms. Slavery was not

abolished in Brazil until 1888, and for the greater part of almost 400 years something like 10,000 slaves a year were imported from Africa. They came from Angola, Congo, Dahoney, Guinea, Mozambique, Nigeria, and West Sudan. Primarily, however, they were from the Mbundu and Ovinbundu tribes of Angola. With them they brought their often sophisticated tribal dances and rhythm instruments. These instruments were largely crude but very effective, comprising various drums, pandeiros (tambourines), chocallos (hollow tubes filled with hard seeds and shaken to give a very special noise), livros (cigar boxes struck with a stick like a drum) and many more, all

The School of Samba procession in the Rio de Janeiro carnival in Brazil

of them inexpensive and very easy to make. They also brought many tribal dances with them, including the Batuque and the Semba. With time these have blended with the Portuguese and native Indian dances to form the dance we now call Samba.

Carnival time

At the heart of Brazilian culture is the exhilarating spectacle of the Mardi Gras carnival in Rio de Janeiro. This happens on each Shrove Tuesday, which is followed the day after by fasting for Lent. Carnival means 'farewell to meat', and is marked with revelry to fortify oneself for the 40 bleak days to come. Nowhere in the world are the festivities marking the event celebrated as much as they are in Brazil. A magnificent parade passes through Rio de Janeiro - everyone dances and wears fantastic costumes and especially huge and flamboyant head-dresses.The actress Carmen Miranda was famous for wearing such head gear.

Fred and Ginger

It was more than 100 years ago, in 1905, that Europe saw any form of Samba. The first form to invade Europe was called the Maxixe. It was featured in George Edward's stage production, *Lady Madcap*. A famous dance couple of the early 20th century, Vernon and Irene Castle, featured the dance in their shows. Vernon was a Briton who had emigrated to New York, where he and his American wife, Irene, became probably the leading dance couple of the era. However, the Maxixe, while related to the Samba, was not its full-blooded ancestor. Signs of what was to come were apparent in the 1933 film

Flying Down to Rio, which featured Fred Astaire and Ginger Rogers dancing together for the first time. The film includes the Carioca, a dance with a Samba influence. Carioca is the name of a small river running through Rio, and Samba dancers often call themselves Cariocas. The real impact of Samba that helped to establish the music and dance came with the films of Carmen Miranda and with the New York World's Fair, in 1939, where the Brazilian Government sent a large number of popular Samba bands.

Samba variations

We say 'the dance' but there are many variations, for example, there is a slow version known as the Baion and a fast version that is more like marching music. It is not surprising that there are so many forms of Samba and the music, when one considers not only the historical background but also the fact that the country is so large. Brazil is more than 34 times larger (and has a population three times greater) than that of the UK, and, excluding Alaska and Hawaii, it is larger than the USA in area.

The hold and dance figures

Most dancers prefer the Open Hold (see pages 14–15) but some find a closer hold suits them better. Samba music is in 2/4 time and, as with all Latin dances, it can be complex but, for beginners, there is no need to be concerned with the more intricate developments of the rhythms. All the figures described are built around a basis of two slow steps to each bar of music. When you have progressed a little more there will, as you might expect, be variations on this simple rhythm.

did you know?

Samba schools

One of the most spectacular aspects of the Rio carnival procession is provided by the 'escolas de samba', or 'samba schools'. Immediately after Mardi Gras the schools start working on a theme and dances for the next year's procession. At the end of the year they compete against each other and are assessed as they each pass a specially erected pavilion called the Sambadrome. Each school comprises the musicians called 'ritmistas', the dancers called 'passistas' and the floats carrying the glamorous women in skimpy costumes with beautiful head adornments.

Left Pendulum

When you have the pattern of the figure clear in your mind, there is a 'bounce action' on the steps, which will improve your enjoyment of the dance. Start with both knees slightly bent, and on each beat of music straighten the legs and knees (though not stiffly) and then bend again. So over the four steps you will also have a pattern of bouncing: up, down, up down, up down, up down. This is a subtle movement and you should take care not to overdo it. It may seem a little daunting but if you learn the figures step-by-step you should not find it very difficult. The characteristic bounce action can be added to all Samba figures in this book.

The steps here are described without turns but when comfortable with the pattern you can turn a little to the left throughout the figure.

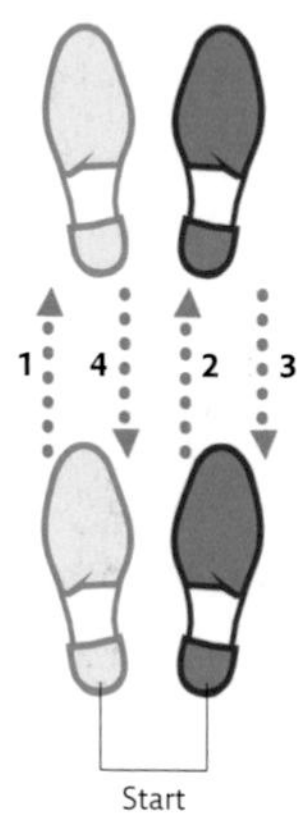

count: **Man's Steps**

one 1 **Left foot** takes a medium step forwards, taking one beat of music.

two 2 **Right foot** closes to left foot, putting a little pressure on right foot but retaining weight on the left foot and taking one beat of music.

one 3 **Right foot** takes a medium step backwards, taking one beat of music.

two 4 **Left foot** closes to right foot, putting a little pressure on the left foot but retaining weight on the right foot and taking one beat of music.

must know

Musical tempo

Samba music is played at various speeds, ranging from a slow Baion to a fast version that is at march tempo and rhythm. The figures described here fit any speed of music you are likely to meet.

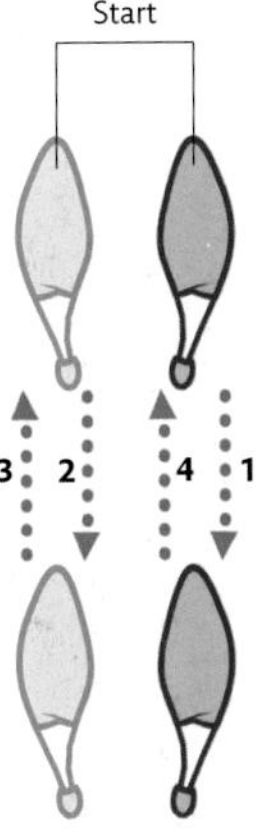

count: **Lady's Steps**

one 1 **Right foot** takes a medium step backwards, taking one beat of music.

two 2 **Left foot** closes to right foot, putting a little pressure on the left foot but retaining weight on the right foot and taking one beat of music.

one 3 **Left foot** takes a medium step forwards, taking one beat of music.

two 4 **Right foot** closes to left foot, putting a little pressure on right foot but retaining weight on the left foot and taking one beat of music.

Left Pendulum

1

count: one

M **Left foot** takes a step forwards.

L **Right foot** takes a step backwards.

Takes one beat of music.

2

count: two

M **Right foot** closes to left foot, retaining weight on left foot.

L **Left foot** closes to right foot, retaining weight on right foot.

Takes one beat of music.

3

count: one

M **Right foot** takes a step backwards.

L **Left foot** takes a step forwards.

Takes one beat of music.

4

count: two

M **Left foot** closes to right foot, retaining weight on right foot.

L **Right foot** closes to left foot, retaining weight on left foot.

Takes one beat of music.

Link and Right Pendulum

Once you have become familiar with the foot patterns, try turning to the right slightly throughout the figure, together with the 'bounce action' described on page 24. Steps 3–6 comprise the Right Pendulum and can be repeated as often as you wish. When you have completed steps 1–6, steps 3 and 4 can be danced again, to allow you to follow this figure with another that commences with the man's left foot and the lady's right foot.

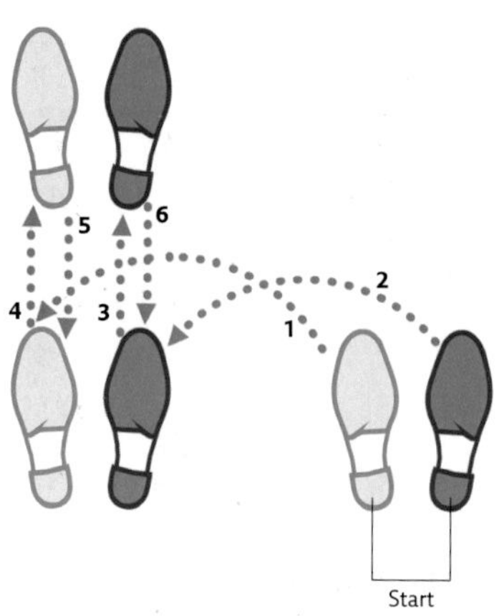

count: **Man's Steps**

one **1 Left foot** takes a step to the side, taking one beat of music.

two **2 Right foot** closes to left foot, putting a little pressure on right foot but retaining weight on left foot and taking one beat of music.

one **3 Right foot** takes a step forwards, taking one beat of music.

two **4 Left foot** closes to right foot, putting a little pressure on left foot but retaining weight on right foot and taking one beat of music.

one **5 Left foot** takes a step backwards, taking one beat of music.

two **6 Right foot** closes to left foot, putting a little pressure on right foot but retaining weight on left foot and taking one beat of music.

must know

Progressive links
This movement is useful when you want to move around the room a little. Face the nearest wall and turn slightly to the left until you are 'facing diagonally to wall', then dance the first four steps of the Link and Right Pendulum, as man and lady, and it will take you along a line generally parallel to wall. The count for this is: side, close, step, close. The steps and the count can be repeated as often as you wish.

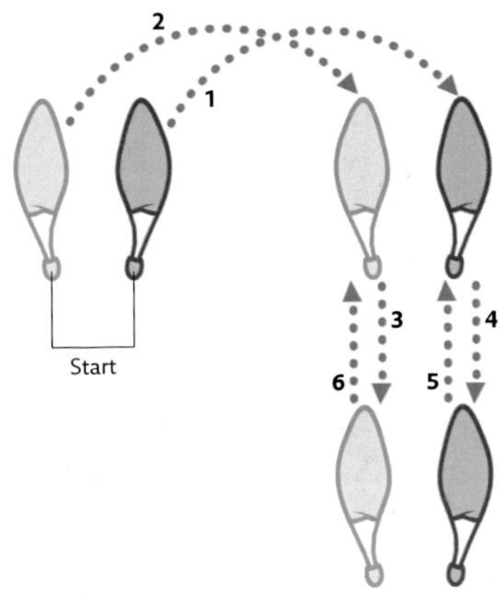

count:

Lady's Steps

one 1 **Right foot** takes a step to the side, taking one beat of music.

two 2 **Left foot** closes to right foot, putting a little pressure on left foot but retaining weight on right foot and taking one beat of music.

one 3 **Left foot** takes a step backwards, taking one beat of music.

two 4 **Right foot** closes to left foot, putting a little pressure on right foot but retaining weight on left foot and taking one beat of music.

one 5 **Right foot** takes a step forwards, taking one beat of music.

two 6 **Left foot** closes to right foot, putting a little pressure on left foot but retaining weight on right foot and taking one beat of music.

Link and Right Pendulum

1

count: one

M **Left foot** takes a step to the side.

L **Right foot** takes a step to the side.

Takes one beat of music.

2

count: two

M **Right foot** closes to left foot, retaining weight on left foot.

L **Left foot** closes to right foot, retaining weight on right foot.

Takes one beat of music.

4

count: two

M **Left foot** closes to right foot, retaining weight on right foot.

L **Right foot** closes to left foot, retaining weight on left foot.

Takes one beat of music.

5

count: one

M **Left foot** takes a step backwards.

L **Right foot** takes a step forwards.

Takes one beat of music.

3

count: one

M **Right foot** takes a step forwards.

L **Left foot** takes a step backwards.

Takes one beat of music.

6

count: two

M **Right foot** closes to left foot, retaining weight on left foot.

L **Left foot** closes to right foot, retaining weight on right foot.

Takes one beat of music.

must know

Like a pendulum

When danced in close hold this figure and similar ones can be enhanced by leaning backwards slightly on forwards steps and forwards on backwards steps. This is where the name Pendulum comes from. In addition it can also be danced with slight turn to the right throughout. You will find this more fulfilling and enjoyable.

Outside Pendulum

This figure gives a little variety to the pendulum action. It consists of the Link and Right Pendulum (see pages 28–31) with the addition of a contrary turn that allows for the lady to step to her left of her partner's body, that is, 'outside partner'.

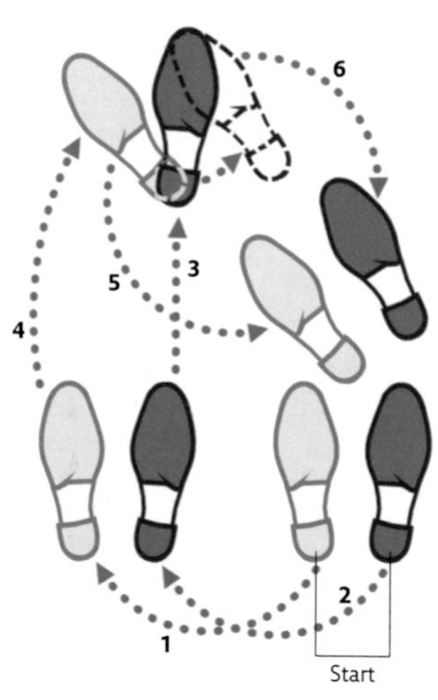

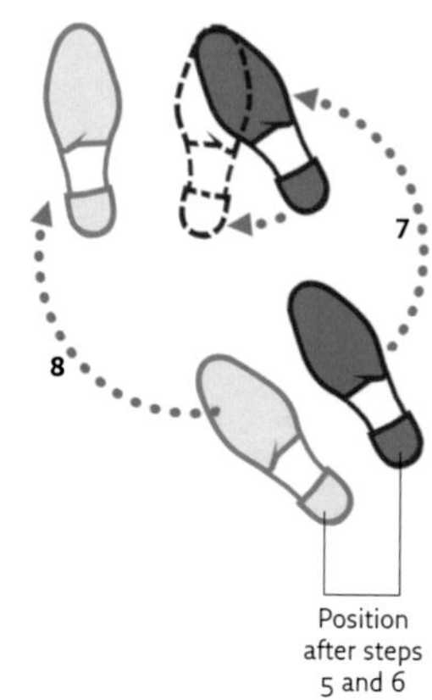

count: **Man's Steps**

one **1 Left foot** takes a step to the side.

two **2 Right foot** closes to left foot, putting a little pressure on right foot but retaining weight on left foot.

one **3 Right foot** takes a step forwards, turning to left. This turn is a little unusual so make sure that you turn towards your left side.

two **4 Left foot** closes to right foot, putting a little pressure on left foot but retaining weight on right foot, still turning left.

one **5 Left foot** takes a step backwards, bringing partner forwards on your right side ('outside partner').

two **6 Right foot** closes to left foot, putting a little pressure on right foot but retaining weight on left foot.

one **7 Right foot** takes a step forwards to your left of your partner's feet ('outside partner'), starting to turn to the right.

two **8 Left foot** closes to right foot, putting a little pressure on left foot but retaining weight on right foot and completing turn to right to finish facing your partner in normal hold.

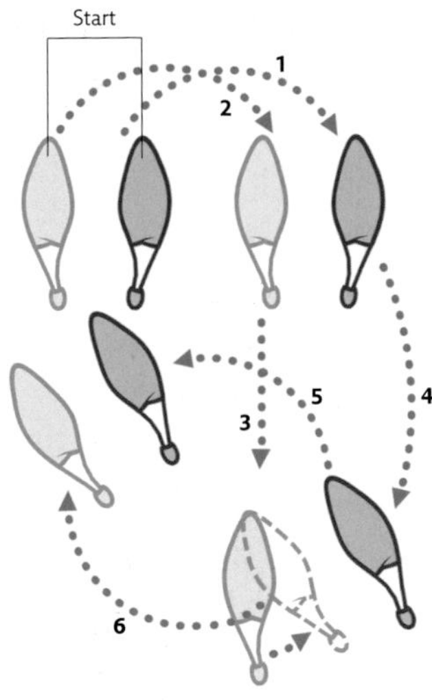

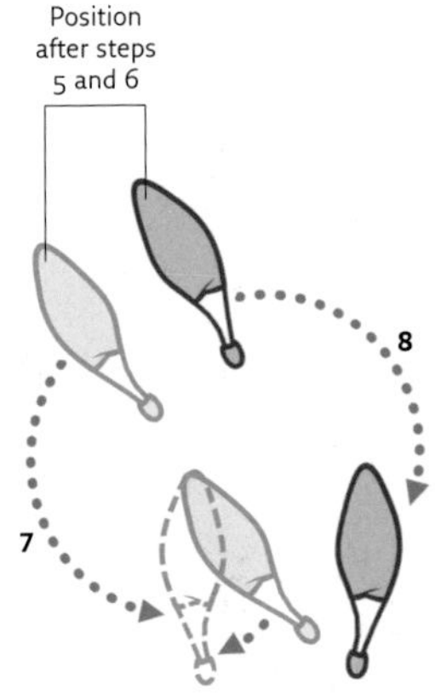

count: **Lady's Steps**

one **1 Right foot** takes a step to the side.

two **2 Left foot** closes to right foot, putting a little pressure on left foot but retaining weight on right foot.

one **3 Left foot** takes a step backwards, turning to left. This turn is a little unusual so make sure that you turn towards your left side.

two **4 Right foot** closes to left foot, putting a little pressure on right foot but retaining weight on left foot, still turning left.

one **5 Right foot** takes a step forwards to your left of your partner ('outside partner').

two **6 Left foot** closes to right foot, putting a little pressure on left foot but retaining weight on right foot.

one **7 Left foot** takes a step backwards with partner stepping to your right side ('outside partner'), starting to turn to the right.

two **8 Right foot** closes to left foot, putting a little pressure on right foot but retaining weight on left foot and completing turn to right to finish facing your partner in normal hold.

Outside Pendulum

1
count: one

M **Left foot** takes a step to the side.

L **Right foot** takes a step to the side.

2
count: two

M **Right foot** closes to left foot, retaining weight on left foot.

L **Left foot** closes to right foot, retaining weight on right foot.

5
count: one

M **Left foot** takes a step backwards, guiding lady to step 'outside partner'.

L **Right foot** takes a step forwards , stepping 'outside partner'.

6
count: two

M **Right foot** closes to left foot, retaining weight on left foot.

L **Left foot** closes to right foot, retaining weight on right foot.

must know

When you feel confident dancing this figure, you can add the bounce action (see page 24).

3

count: one

M **Right foot** takes a step forwards, turning to the left.

L **Left foot** takes a step backwards, turning to the left.

4

count: two

M **Left foot** closes to right foot, retaining weight on right foot.

L **Right foot** closes to left foot, retaining weight on left foot.

Both still turning left.

7

count: one

M **Right foot** takes a step forwards, 'outside partner', starting to turn to the right.

L **Left foot** takes a step backwards, starting to turn to the right.

8

count: two

M **Left foot** closes to right foot, completing turn to right.

L **Right foot** closes to left foot, completing turn to right to finish facing partner.

Samba Whisks

This figure is fun and is a means of turning into the promenade position, where the man's left and the lady's right side pull away from each other so that their bodies make a V pattern when viewed from above. This allows them to step forwards together using the open side of the V, after step 4.

Steps 1–4 can be repeated several times before dancing steps 5 and 6.

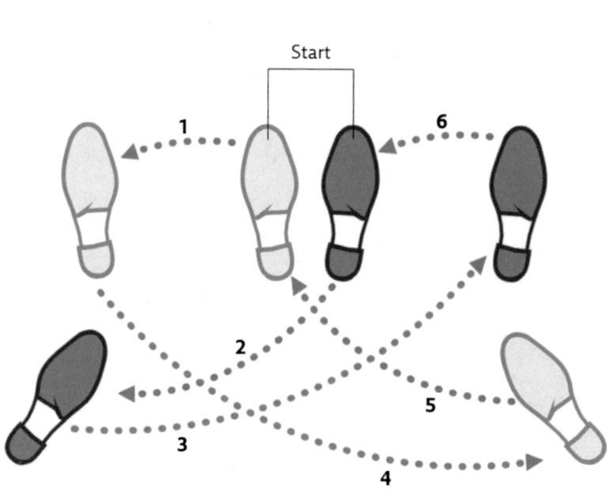

count:

Man's Steps

one 1 **Left foot** takes a step to the side.

two 2 **Right foot** crosses loosely behind left foot, putting slight pressure on the toes of right foot. Give the lady a push with the heel of your right hand, but do not push forwards with the left hand. This should cause her to turn left and finish with her left side away from you.

one 3 **Right foot** takes a step to the side, pushing on partner's right hand with your left hand turning her to normal position to face you.

two 4 **Left foot** crosses loosely behind right foot, putting slight pressure on the toes of left foot. Increase the pressure of the right hand on the lady's back and push forwards a little with the left hand. These hand actions should cause the lady to turn her right side away from you.

one 5 **Left foot** takes a step to the side, turning your partner to face you, relaxing pressure with right hand and pulling left hand back slightly.

two 6 **Right foot** closes to left foot, putting slight pressure on the toes of your right foot.

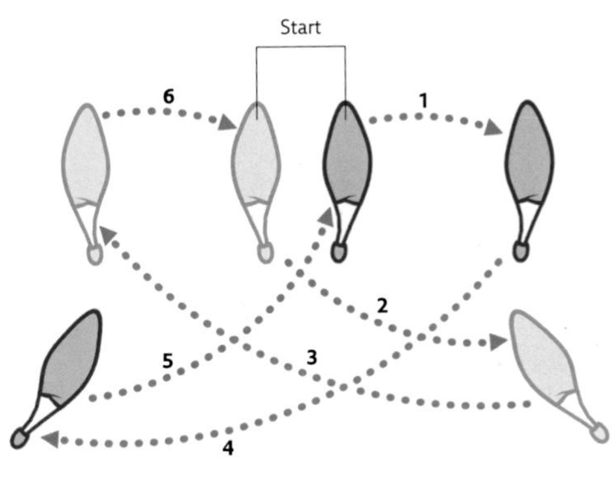

count:

Lady's Steps

one **1 Right foot** takes a step to the side.

two **2 Left foot** crosses loosely behind right foot, putting slight pressure on the toes of left foot. Your partner will lead you to turn your body to your left and finish with your left side away from him, try not to resist him but go along with the guidance.

one **3 Left foot** takes a step to the side, turning to face partner in normal position (partner should have led you into the position).

two **4 Right foot** crosses loosely behind left foot, putting slight pressure on the toes of right foot. Your partner will push your right hand backwards.These hand actions should guide you to turn your right side away from partner.

one **5 Right foot** takes a step to the side, turning to face partner. The pressure from the man's right hand has been relaxed.

two **6 Left foot** closes to right foot, putting slight pressure on the toes of your left foot.

Samba Whisks

1

count: one

M Left foot takes a step to the side.

L Right foot takes a step to the side.

2

count: two

M Right foot crosses loosely behind left foot. Gently push lady with right hand so she turns.

L Left foot crosses loosely behind right foot, turning to your left.

4

count: two

M Left foot crosses loosely behind right foot. Increase pressure of right hand on lady's back.

L Right foot crosses loosely behind left foot, turning to right side.

5

count: one

M Left foot to the side turning partner to face you, pulling your left hand back slightly.

L Right foot to the side, turning to face partner.

3

count: one

M Right foot to the side, turning partner by pushing on her right hand with your left hand.

L Left foot to the side, turning to face partner.

6

count: two

M Right foot closes to left foot putting slight pressure on right foot.

L Left foot closes to right foot, putting slight pressure on left foot.

want to know more?

- Try some simple Salsa next, see pages 106–35.
- Try dancing the figures with different partners.
- Practise dancing the figures in rooms of any size or shape.
- Join a dance school. For addresses, look in local newspapers, Yellow Pages and see Dance studios on pages 184–9.
- Check with your local authority for evening classes.
- Watch the film *Flying Down to Rio*, starring Fred Astaire and Ginger Rogers, for inspiration.

weblinks

- For dance history, videos and DVDs, visit www.centralhome.com/ballroomcountry/samba
- For more information on Samba from around the world visit www.worldsamba.org
- See pages 183–4 for websites of dance teachers' organisations.

3 Rumba

Dance, like everything else in life, develops and changes with time. The present Rumba is the descendent of the Cuban dances, the Son and Danson, and, while it still has many elements of those dances, it is more in keeping with today's environment. It is the slowest of the Latin dances and is stylish, subtle, syncopated and sophisticated. It is the favourite of most good Latin dancers and, as befits the dance, is probably the most difficult to express adequately. However, the figures included in this section are simple enough for you to attempt and enjoy.

A classic Latin dance

Rumba is the common name for the dance of Cuba but it is a misnomer because there is no one dance, there are many. The Cha Cha Cha and Salsa are also derived from the Rumba.

As with all Caribbean music and dances, the primary influence came from African slaves in the four-and-a-half centuries following the first discovery of America and the annexation of Cuba for Spain by Christopher Columbus in 1492. The Spaniards established sugar plantations in Cuba, which needed a great many workers to produce the sugar. The native Cubans were sparse in numbers and the diseases carried by the conquerors, such as measles, were devastating to the native population who had never before been exposed to these diseases. The death toll was immense and labour was needed. It was supplied by slaves brought mainly from the west coast of Africa.

The slaves brought their native traditions of music and dance with them while the Spaniards brought the dances of Spain and Europe. Contradanzas and Waltzes were just two European dances that found their way into the dance salons of Cuba.

must know

Rumba steps

All steps are taken on the ball of the foot first and then the weight is allowed to settle over the foot, while the supporting leg straightens causing the hips to settle sideways. This is explained in the Basic Movement (see pages 44–7) and, although it is not repeated, it takes place throughout the dance.

Musical accompaniment

The musical instruments of these countries also came to Cuba. From Spain came the guitar and castanets, while from Africa came the various drums, including bongos with the two differently toned drums, the maracas – roughly an egg-shaped sphere filled with dried beads on a handle – and the claves. The claves are two hard wood sticks that are beaten together to give a particular clicking noise that is used to set and maintain the tempo.

A group of dancers demonstrate the Rumba at the Nautilus Bath Club in Miami, Florida in 1932.

They are normally played in a syncopated two-bar phrase and American band leaders taught their singers to use them by getting them to say, to themselves, 'shave, haircut, two bits'. Over a two-bar phrase of 4/4 music the accents fall on the 1st, 4th, 7th quaver in the first bar and on the 3rd and 5th quaver in the second bar. While other syncopated rhythms are now used regularly, this traditional two-bar phrase is still almost always evident.

Rhythmic patterns

In a dance where the music has such complex rhythmic patterns, the counting for the steps is not entirely straightforward. The forwards step of the basic figures commences on the second crotchet in the bar of music. However, because the melody phrases in the tunes often start on the first crotchet, some beginners find the second beat rhythm a little difficult. At this stage do not worry about this, concentrate on the foot patterns.

There are many similarities between Rumba, Cha Cha Cha and Salsa, and nearly all figures with slight amendments can be transferred from one rhythm to another in this trio of dances.

must know

The hold

For basic Rumba figures use an Open Hold (see pages 14–15).

The Basic Movement

This figure is similar to the basic figure in Cha Cha Cha (see pages 76–9). In this Basic Movement you should make a small turn to the left throughout, once you have mastered the steps. Over one full figure turn a quarter of a full turn, that is, if you start with your back to the nearest wall you should have your left shoulder facing the same wall at the end of one full basic figure.

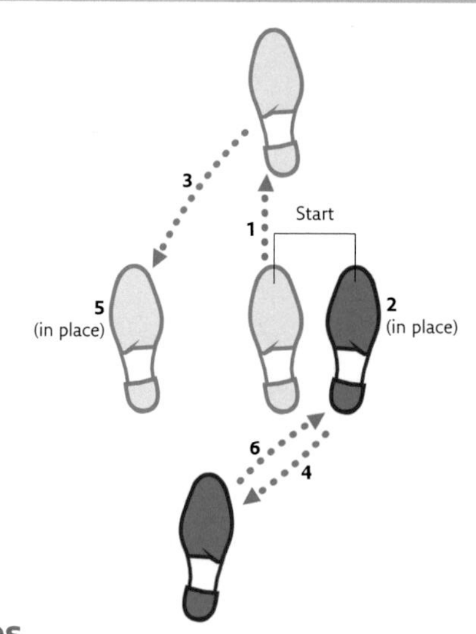

count: **Man's Steps**

two 1 Left foot takes a small step forwards on the ball of the foot, taking weight onto flat foot at the end of the step and swinging hips to the left. Takes one beat of music.

three 2 Right foot remains in place and weight transfers onto it, swinging hips to the right. Takes one beat of music.

four-one 3 Left foot takes a step to the side on the ball of the foot and, as weight transfers onto foot, swinging hips to the left. Takes two beats of music.

two 4 Right foot takes a small step backwards and, as weight transfers onto it, lift the heel of your left foot a little off the floor, swinging hips to the right. Takes one beat of music.

three 5 Left foot remains in place, lowering heel as weight is taken forwards onto it and swinging hips to the left. Takes one beat of music.

four-one 6 Right foot takes a step to the side on ball of foot and, as weight transfers onto foot, swinging hips to the right. Takes two beats of music.

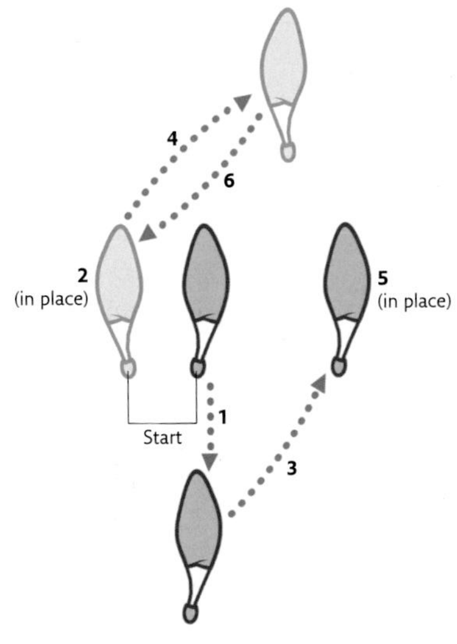

count:

Lady's Steps

two 1 Right foot takes a small step backwards and, as weight transfers onto it, lift the heel of your left foot a little off the floor, swinging hips to the right. Takes one beat of music.

three 2 Left foot remains in place, lowering heel as weight is taken forwards onto it and swinging hips to the left. Takes one beat of music.

four-one 3 Right foot takes a step to the side on the ball of the foot and, as weight transfers onto foot, swinging hips to the right. Takes two beats of music.

two 4 Left foot takes a small step forwards on the ball of the foot, taking weight onto flat foot at the end of the step, swinging hips to the left. Takes one beat of music.

three 5 Right foot remains in place and weight transfers onto it, swinging hips to the right. Takes one beat of music.

four-one 6 Left foot takes a step to the side on the ball of the foot and, as weight transfers onto foot, swinging hips to the left. Takes two beats of music.

The Basic Movement

1

count: two

M Left foot takes a step forwards, swinging hips to the left.

L Right foot takes a step backwards, swinging hips to the right.

Takes one beat of music.

2

count: three

M Right foot remains in place, weight back onto it, hips to the right.

L Left foot remains in place, weight forwards onto it, hips to the left.

Takes one beat of music.

4

count: two

M Right foot takes a step backwards, swinging hips to the right.

L Left foot takes a step forwards, swinging hips to the left.

Takes one beat of music.

5

count: three

M Left foot remains in place, weight forwards onto it, hips to the left.

L Right foot remains in place, weight back onto it, hips to the right.

Takes one beat of music.

3

count: four-one

M **Left foot** takes a step to the side, swinging hips to the left.

L **Right foot** takes a step to the side, swinging hips to the right.

Takes two beats of music.

6

count: four-one

M **Right foot** takes a step to the side, swinging hips to the right.

L **Left foot** takes a step to the side, swinging hips to the left.

Takes two beats of music.

did you know?

Cuban bands

Rumba music was first popularised in Britain by the recordings of the Lecuona Cuban Boys and the band of Don Azpiazu, which toured Britain and Europe in the mid 1930s with considerable success. Ernesto Lecuona was not only a popular band leader but also a serious classical musician.

Side Cucarachas

Dance this figure after the Basic Movement (see pages 44-7) and then follow it with the Basic Movement.

As you become more familiar with the Rumba figures you will see that Side Cucarachas can precede any of them.

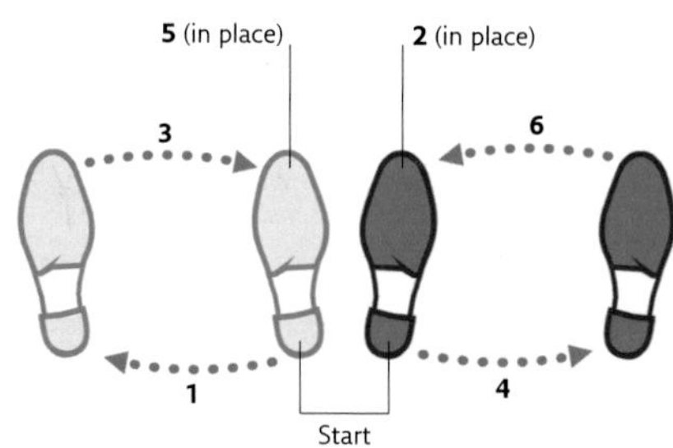

count: **Man's Steps**

two 1 **Left foot** takes a step to the side, pressing foot into floor so as to lever weight of body into next step.

three 2 **Right foot** remains in place and full weight is taken onto it.

four-one 3 **Left foot** closes to right foot.

two 4 **Right foot** takes a step to the side, pressing foot into floor so as to lever weight of body into next step.

three 5 **Left foot** remains in place and full weight is taken onto it.

four-one 6 **Right foot** closes to left foot.

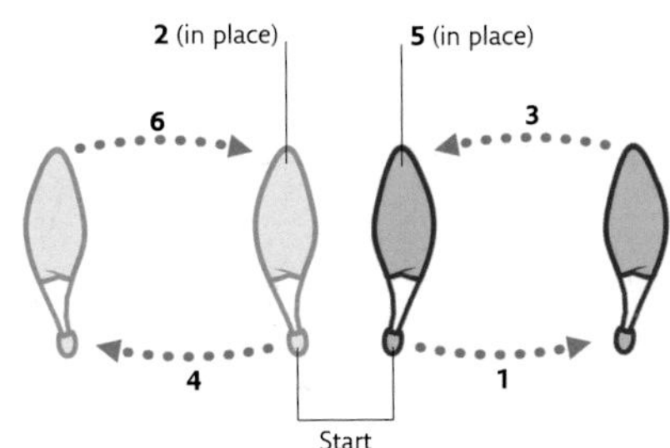

Lady's Steps

count:

- **two** 1 Right foot foot takes a step to the side, pressing foot into floor so as to lever weight of body into next step.
- **three** 2 Left foot remains in place and full weight is taken onto it.
- **four-one** 3 Right foot closes to left foot.
- **two** 4 Left foot takes a step to the side, pressing foot into floor so as to lever weight of body into next step.
- **three** 5 Right foot remains in place and full weight is taken onto it.
- **four-one** 6 Left foot closes to right foot.

must know

Body language

The movement of the hips from side to side, as described in the Basic Movement on pages 44–7, is a vital part of this figure. In order to get the best out of it, you will need to keep your waist loose and fluid. However, keep your head and shoulders steady.

Side Cucarachas

1

count: two

M Left foot to side, with pressure, so as to lever weight into next step.

L Right foot to side, pressing into floor so as to lever weight into next step.

2

count: three

M Right foot remains in place and full weight is taken onto it.

L Left foot remains in place and full weight is taken onto it.

4

count: two

M Right foot to side, with pressure so as to lever weight into next step.

L Left foot to side, pressing into floor so as to lever weight into next step.

5

count: three

M Left foot remains in place and full weight is taken onto it.

L Right foot remains in place and full weight taken onto it.

3
count:four-one

M **Left foot** closes to right foot.

L **Right foot** closes to left foot.

6
count: four-one

M **Right foot** closes to left foot.

L **Left foot** closes to right foot.

The Opening Outs

This figure, danced in the Open Hold (see pages 14–15), is a variation on the Side Cucarachas (see pages 48–51).

Like Cucarachas, the Opening Outs can also follow and be followed by the Basic Movement (see pages 44–7).

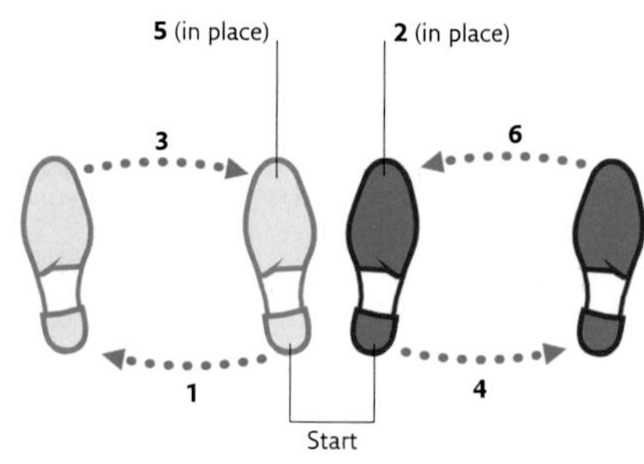

count: **Man's Steps**

two 1 **Left foot** takes a step to the side, using pressure into the floor, and pushing your partner with the left hand and then releasing hold.

three 2 **Right foot** remains in place and full weight is taken onto it, guiding the lady to step forwards.

four-one 3 **Left foot** closes to right foot, your partner turns to face you and you regain hold of her right hand with your left hand.

two 4 **Right foot** takes a step to the side, using pressure into the floor, and pushing your partner with the right hand and then releasing hold.

three 5 **Left foot** remains in place and full weight is taken onto it, guiding the lady to step forwards.

four-one 6 **Right foot** closes to left foot, partner turns to face you. Regain normal hold.

must know

Good lead

The man's lead to the lady must be firm and positive and the lady must release the hold she has of the man's hand as soon as she feels the lead. It is good if both man and lady can hold their free hand in a relaxed manner without stiff fingers or clenched fist.

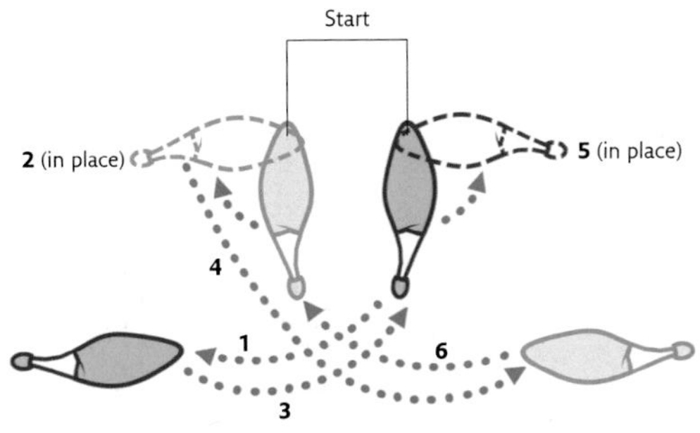

Lady's Steps

count:

two 1 **Right foot** takes a step backwards, using pressure into the floor, and before turning about 90 degrees to the right and releasing hold of partner's hand from your right hand.

three 2 **Left foot** remains in place and full weight is taken forwards onto it.

four-one 3 **Right foot** takes a step to the side, turning to the left to face your partner and regain hold of his left hand with your right hand.

two 4 **Left foot** takes a step backwards, using pressure into the floor, and before turning about 90 degrees to the left and releasing hold of partner from left hand.

three 5 **Right foot** remains in place and full weight is taken forwards onto it.

four-one 6 **Left foot** takes a step to the side, turning to the right to face your partner. Regain normal hold.

The Opening Outs

must know

Pizazz!

When you are sure of the steps in this figure the man can add more zest to it by turning to the left on step 1 and turning to the right to face his partner on steps 2 and 3. He can then turn to the right on step 4 and turn to the left to face partner on steps 5 and 6.

1

count: two

M Left foot to side, guiding partner with left hand and then release hold.

L Right foot backwards, turning about 90 degrees to the right.

4

count: two

M Right foot to side, guiding partner with right hand and then release hold.

L Left foot backwards, turning about 90 degrees to the left .

2

count: three

M Right foot remains in place, weight is taken onto it, leading lady to step forwards.

L Left foot remains in place and full weight is taken onto it.

3

count: four-one

M Left foot closes to right foot, regaining hold of partner's right hand.

L Right foot to side, turning to left to face partner and regain hold of his hand.

5

count: three

M Left foot remains in place and weight is taken onto it, guiding the lady to step forwards.

L Right foot remains in place and full weight is taken onto it.

6

count: four-one

M Right foot closes to left foot, turning partner to face you and regain normal hold.

L Left foot to side turning to right to face partner.

The New York

Prior to dancing this figure check the left turn on step 6 of the Basic Movement (see pages 44–7). The man prepares to turn right and will have started to turn the lady a little to her left. You are now in a good position for the New York. This figure can also be followed by the Basic Movement.

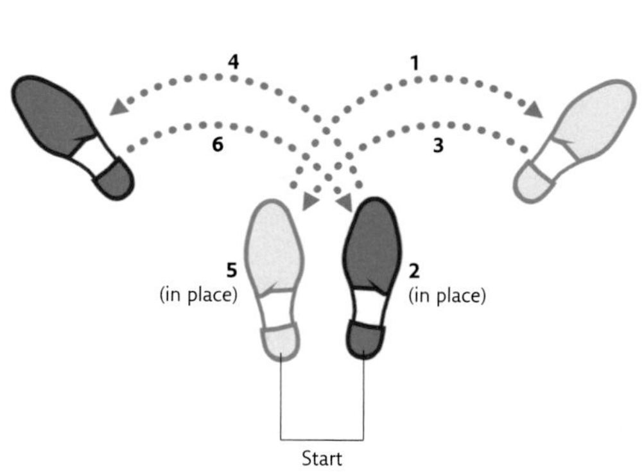

count: **Man's Steps**

two **1** **Left foot** steps forwards and across the right foot, releasing hold of your partner with your right hand. Lady steps forwards with you in open counter promenade position.

three **2** **Right foot** remains in place and weight is taken back onto it, starting to turn left.

four-one **3** **Left foot** takes a step to the side, turning to the left to face your partner, taking hold of her left hand in your right and releasing hold of her right hand from your left hand.

two **4** **Right foot** forwards and across the left foot. The lady is stepping forwards with you in open promenade position.

three **5** **Left foot** remains in place and weight is taken back onto it, starting to turn to right.

four-one **6** **Right foot** takes a step to the side, turning to the right to face your partner, regaining normal hold of her with her right hand in your left and your right hand on her back.

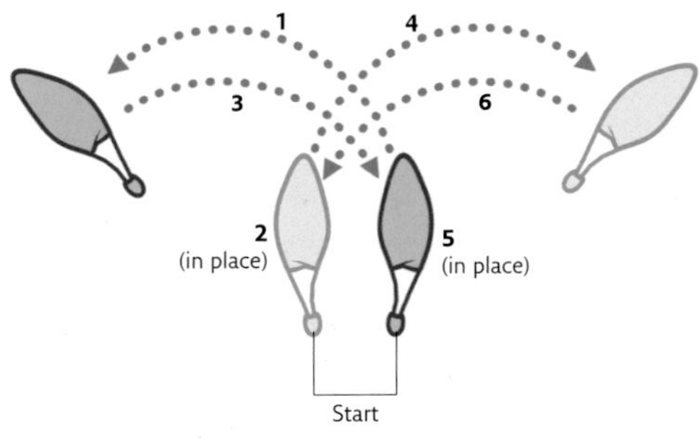

count: **Lady's Steps**

two **1** **Right foot** steps forwards and across the left foot. The man will release hold of you with his right hand, bring your left hand up to shoulder level in open counter promenade position.

three **2** **Left foot** remains in place and weight is taken back onto it, starting to turn right.

four-one **3** **Right foot** takes a step to the side, turning to the right to face partner. Partner will release hold of your right hand from his left and at the same time take your left hand in his right.

two **4** **Left foot** takes a step forwards and across the right foot. The man is stepping forwards with you in open promenade position.

three **5** **Right foot** remains in place and weight is taken back onto it, starting to turn to left.

four-one **6** **Left foot** takes a step to the side, turning to the left to face partner, regaining normal hold of partner.

The New York

1

count: two

M Left foot forwards and across right foot, releasing hold with right hand.

L Right foot forwards and across left foot in open counter promenade position.

must know

Hip action
Remember that throughout all the Rumba figures, steps are taken on the ball of the foot first and then the weight settles over the foot, while the supporting leg straightens causing the hips to settle sideways.

4

count: two

M Right foot forwards and across left foot, in open promenade position.

L Left foot forwards and across right foot in open promenade position.

2

count: three

M **Right foot** remains in place, weight back onto it, starting to turn left.

L **Left foot** remains in place, weight back onto it, starting to turn right.

3

count: four-one

M **Left foot** to side, turn to face partner, take hold of her left hand, let go of her right hand.

L **Right foot** to side, turning to right to face partner.

5

count: three

M **Left foot** remains in place, weight back onto it, starting to turn right.

L **Right foot** remains in place and weight back onto it, starting to turn left.

6

count: four-one

M **Right foot** to side, turning to face partner, regaining normal hold.

L **Left foot** to side, turning to left to face partner, regaining normal hold.

The Fan

Steps 1-3 of the Basic Movement (see page 44-7) are included here, in order to create a composite learning unit. In the Fan, which comprises steps 4-6, the man turns the lady so that her body is at right angles to his. Follow this complete figure with the Hockey Stick (see pages 64-7).

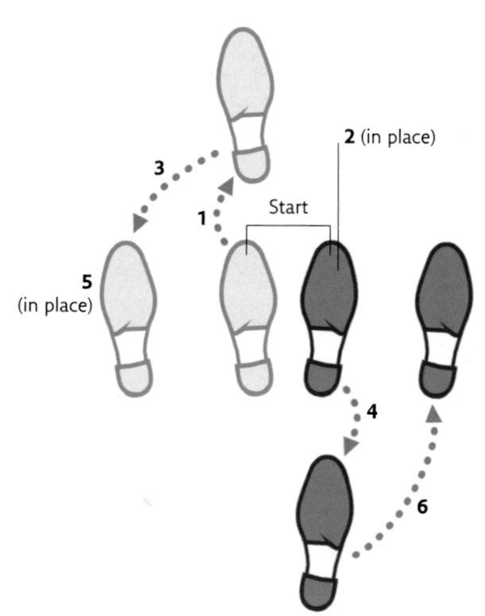

count: **Man's Steps**

two 1 **Left foot** takes a small step forwards.

three 2 **Right foot** remains in place and the weight is taken back onto it.

four-one 3 **Left foot** takes a step to the side, turning slightly to the left and lowering your left hand.

two 4 **Right foot** takes a step backwards, leading the lady to step across and in front of you.

three 5 **Left foot** remains in place and the weight is taken forwards onto it, turning the lady to her left by pulling your left hand back and pushing her with your right hand and then releasing hold of her with that hand.

four-one 6 **Right foot** takes a small step to the side, turning a little to the left to finish at right angles to your partner and almost at arm's length.

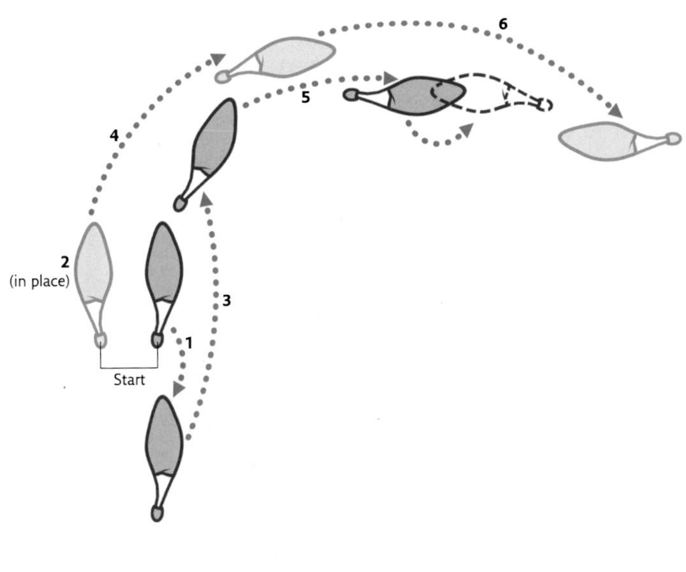

count:

Lady's Steps

two 1 **Right foot** takes a small step backwards.

three 2 **Left foot** remains in place and the weight is taken forwards onto it.

four-one 3 **Right foot** takes a step to the side, turning slightly to the right and lowering your right hand.

two 4 **Left foot** takes a step forwards across in front of the man.

three 5 **Right foot** takes a step forwards, turning to the left on the ball of your foot, to finish with right foot back. The man will guide you into the turn and then release hold of you from his right hand.

four-one 6 **Left foot** takes a step backwards, still turning to finish at right angles to your partner and almost at arm's length.

The Fan

1

count: two

M Left foot takes a step forwards.

L Right foot takes a step backwards.

2

count: three

M Right foot remains in place and weight is taken back onto it.

L Left foot remains in place and weight is taken forwards onto it.

4

count: two

M Right foot takes a step backwards, leading lady to step across and in front of you.

L Left foot takes a step forwards in front of man.

5

count: three

M Left foot remains in place, weight is taken onto it, turn lady to her left and release hold.

L Right foot takes a step forwards, turning left to end with right foot back.

3

count: four-one

M Left foot steps to side, turning slightly to left and lowering left hand.

L Right foot steps to side, turning slightly to right and lowering right hand.

must know

Essential

The eye contact between couples is an inherent part of the Rumba. And the erect carriage of the trunk along with the lateral movement of the hips are also essential ingredients.

6

count: four-one

M Right foot steps to side turning a little to left.

L Left foot backwards, still turning to finish at right angles to the man and almost at arm's length.

The Hockey Stick

Precede the Hockey Stick with the Fan (see pages 60–3). At the end you are left slightly apart from your partner with the man holding the lady's right hand in his left hand. To regain normal hold, dance the first half of the Basic Movement (see pages 44–7); the man should pull the lady gently towards him.

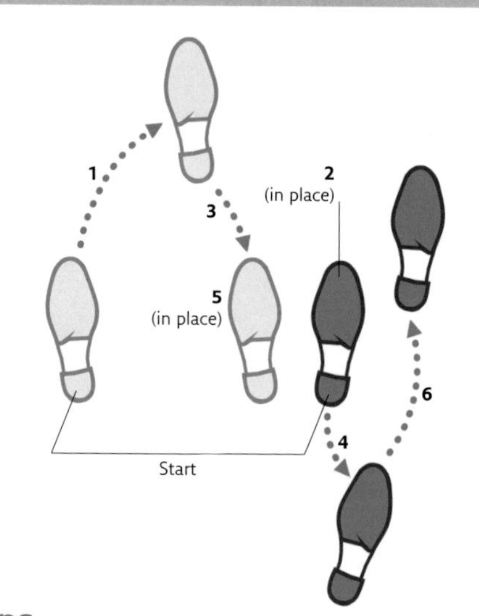

count: **Man's Steps**

two 1 **Left foot** takes a step forwards, keeping left hand relaxed so that lady can close her right foot to left foot.

three 2 **Right foot** remains in place and the weight is taken back onto it, leading the lady to start moving forwards with your left hand.

four-one 3 **Left foot** closes to right foot, still leading the lady forwards (the 90 degree angle between you at end of the Fan means the lady will move in front of you). Raise your left and the lady's right hand to form an arch.

two 4 **Right foot** takes a step backwards, turning slightly to the right and turning the lady to her left with an anti-clockwise movement of your left hand. Do not grip her hand tightly, allowing it to turn in yours.

three 5 **Left foot** remains in place and the weight is taken forwards onto it, still turning the lady and allowing your hand to lower down to just above waist level.

four-one 6 **Right foot** steps forwards towards partner with left hand lowered.

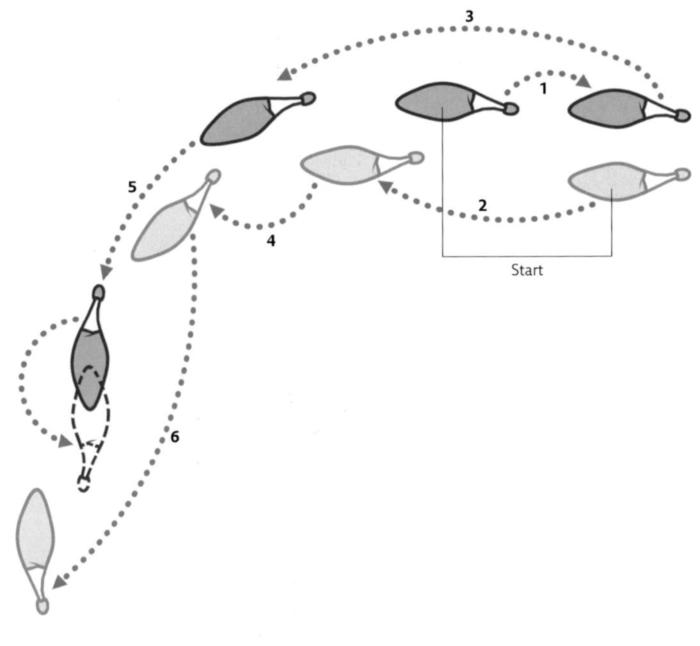

Lady's Steps

count:

two 1 Right foot closes to left foot, remaining slightly away from the man on this step.

three 2 Left foot takes a step forwards, starting to move across and in front of the man.

four-one 3 Right foot takes a step forwards across the front of the man. The man raises your right hand so that you both form an arch for you to turn under.

two 4 Left foot takes a step forwards, starting to turn left under the arch formed by your right and the man's left arms.

three 5 Right foot takes a step forwards, turning left on the ball of your foot to face partner, to finish with right foot back and his left hand holding your right at waist level.

four-one 6 Left foot takes a small step backwards.

The Hockey Stick

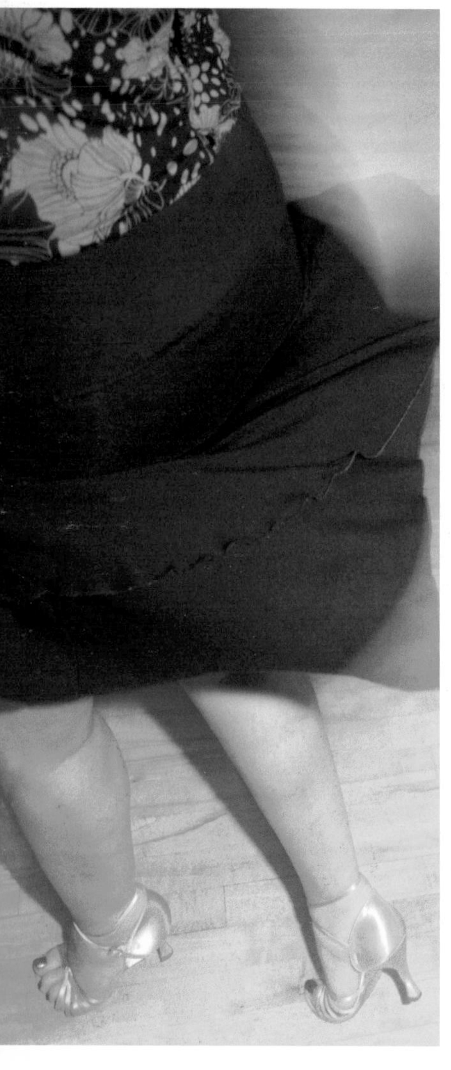

1

count: two

M Left foot takes a step forwards, keeping left hand relaxed.

L Right foot closes to left foot.

4

count: two

M Right foot backwards, turning slightly to the right and turning lady to her left.

L Left foot takes a step forwards, start turning left under the arch.

2

count: three

M **Right foot** remains in place, weight taken back onto it, leading lady to start moving forwards.

L **Left foot** takes a step forwards, starting to move in front of man.

3

count: four-one

M **Left foot** closes to right foot, still leading lady forwards, raising left hand to form an arch.

L **Right foot** forwards in front of man.

5

count: three

M **Left foot** remains in place, weight is taken forwards onto it, still turning lady.

L **Right foot** forwards, turning left to end with right foot back.

6

count: four-one

M **Right foot** takes a step forwards towards partner, lowering left hand.

L **Left foot** takes a small step backwards.

Natural Top

In this figure the man and lady circle around a central point as though they were moving around the rim of and at opposite sides of a wheel. Commence after step 3 of the Basic Movement (see pages 44–7), but make the turn slightly to the right. The close hold (see pages 14–15) is retained throughout and the Natural Top can be followed by steps 4–6 of the Basic Movement.

Once you have mastered the foot pattern, you can increase the amount of turn as shown in the step-by-step photographs.

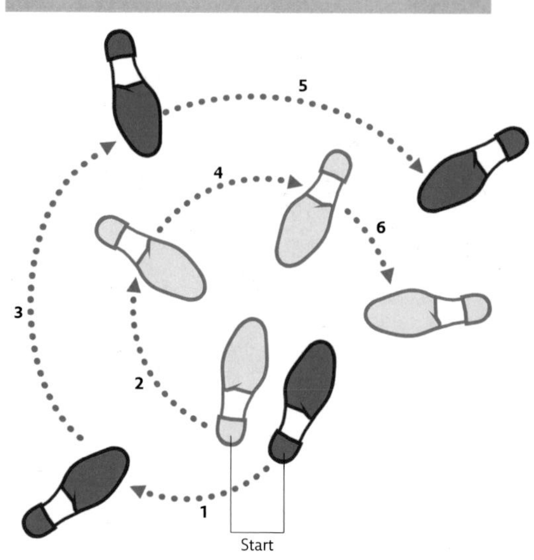

count: **Man's Steps**

two **1** **Right foot** crosses behind left foot placing right toe near to left heel, turning strongly to the right.

three **2** **Left foot** steps to the side and slightly forwards, still turning to the right.

four-one **3** **Right foot** crosses behind left foot, placing right toe near to left heel, turning strongly to the right.

two **4** **Left foot** steps to the side and slightly forwards, still turning to the right.

three **5** **Right foot** crosses behind left foot, placing right toe near to left heel, turning strongly to the right.

four-one **6** **Left foot** steps to the side and slightly forwards, completing the turn to the right.

watch out!

With experience you will find that you can turn quite quickly in this figure, indeed, enough for the centrifugal force to exert quite a pressure on dancers. Both man and lady need to ensure that their hold of their partner is firm enough to control this force.

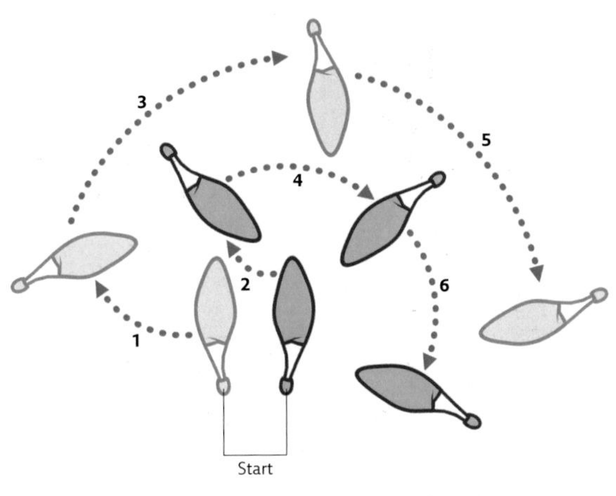

count: **Lady's Steps**

two **1 Left foot** takes a step to the side and slightly backwards, starting to turn strongly to the right.

three **2 Right foot** forwards and across left foot, still turning to the right.

four-one **3 Left foot** steps to the side and slightly backwards, still turning to the right.

two **4 Right foot** forwards and across left foot, still turning to the right.

three **5 Left foot** steps to the side and slightly backwards, still turning to the right.

four-one **6 Right foot** forwards and across left foot, completing the turn to the right.

Natural Top

1

count: two

M Right foot crosses behind left foot placing right toe near to left heel, turning strongly to right.

L Left foot to side and backwards, starting to turn strongly to right.

2

count: three

M Left foot to side and slightly forwards, still turning to right.

L Right foot forwards and across left foot, still turning to right.

4

count: two

M Left foot to side and slightly forwards, still turning to right.

L Right foot forwards and across left foot, still turning to right.

5

count: three

M Right foot crosses behind left foot placing right toe near to left heel, turning strongly to right.

L Left foot to side and slightly backwards, still turning to right.

3

count: four-one

M Right foot crosses behind left foot placing right toe near to left heel, turning strongly to right.

L Left foot side and slightly backwards, still turning to right.

6

count: four-one

M Left foot to side, completing the turn to the right.

L Right foot forwards and across left foot, completing the turn to the right.

want to know more?

- Try the steps to Rumba music played at different speeds.
- Join a local dance school. For addresses look in local newspapers, Yellow Pages, and see Dance studios listed on pages 184-9.
- Set yourself an objective of entering an amateur medal test.
- Get inspired, see the film *Rumba*, starring George Raft and Carol Lombard.

weblinks

- Find out more about competitive ballroom latin dancing, visit www.dancesport.uk
- For dance history, CDs, videos and DVDs visit en.wikipedia.org/wiki/Rumba or www.centralhome.com/ballroomcountry/rumba
- Consult the websites of the dance teachers' organizations (see pages 183-4).

4 Cha Cha Cha

The Cha Cha Cha is directly related to the Rumba but is more lively, with its triple syncopated dance unit from which the dance gets its name. While dancers of all standards will enjoy the dance, the fun aspect makes it more appealing to the less experienced dancer. However, skill is needed and the dancer must be light on his or her feet to express the bubbly rhythms. Good leads from the man to the lady are vital, while the lady needs to respond readily to the guidance from the man.

Cuban roots

Cuban music and dance has had an enormous impact on dancing throughout the world. Three of the dances in this book – Salsa, Rumba and Cha Cha Cha – are Cuban in origin.

The Cha Cha Cha came to prominence in the 1950s. Here two dancers from the famous Arthur Murray Dance School (established in the 1930s and still going today in the USA) practise the dance.

For several years Cha Cha Cha has been the most popular of the Latin American dances, although Salsa has probably now overtaken it. Like Salsa, the Cha Cha Cha has Cuban roots, however, the dance has also been heavily influenced by the American music scene.

As in all dances, response to the music is vital, and you should try to get some good Cuban recordings and note the repeated patterns of the rhythm. In Cha Cha Cha you should listen out for the triplet of beats that occurs around the end of each bar of music. It is quick and the sound 'de de dah' is what you should be listening for.

Whenever you hear the 'de de dah' (Cha Cha Cha) rhythmic break, you should be fitting three steps to that rhythm. These are the basis of the Cha Cha Chah. (Note the last beat is Chah with an 'h.')

The hold

In this dance use the Open Hold (see pages 14–15) – the classic hold for Latin dancing.

All figures in the Cha Cha Cha do not move around the room and can be commenced facing in any direction. However, to start with, the man should try facing the nearest wall and the lady should face him. Basic footwork involves stepping on the ball of your foot first, then lowering the rest of your foot.

Cha Cha Cha starter pattern

Some beginners find the rhythm a little tricky and it will help to put you on the correct beat if you begin with the following starter pattern, which includes a preparatory step taken on the first beat of the bar of music.

P

(one beat of music)

M Left foot marks time in place.

L Right foot marks time in place.

1

count:step

(one beat of music)

M Right foot marks time in place.

L Left foot marks time in place.

2

count: step

(one beat of music)

M Left foot marks time in place.

L Right foot marks time in place.

3

count: cha

(half a beat of music)

M Right foot takes a small step to the side.

L Left foot takes a small step to the side.

4

count: cha

(half a beat of music)

M Left foot closes towards right foot.

L Right foot closes towards left foot.

5

count: chah

(one beat of music)

M Right foot takes a small step to the side.

L Left foot takes a small step to the side.

Forwards and Backwards Cha Cha Cha Basics

This figure can follow the Starter Pattern on page 75.

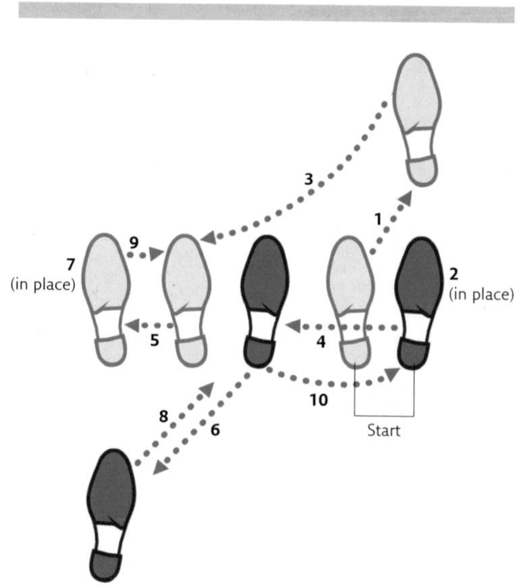

count: **Man's Steps**

step 1 **Left foot** takes a step forwards, taking one beat of music.

step 2 **Right foot** remains in place with the weight taken back onto it, taking one beat of music.

cha 3 **Left foot** takes a step to the side, taking half a beat of music.

cha 4 **Right foot** closes towards but not up to left foot, taking half a beat of music.

chah 5 **Left foot** takes a step to the side, taking one beat of music.

step 6 **Right foot** takes a step backwards, taking one beat of music.

step 7 **Left foot** remains in place with the weight taken forwards onto it, taking one beat of music.

cha 8 **Right foot** takes a step to the side, taking half a beat of music.

cha 9 **Left foot** closes towards but not up to right foot, taking half a beat of music.

chah 10 **Right foot** takes a small step to the side, taking one beat of music.

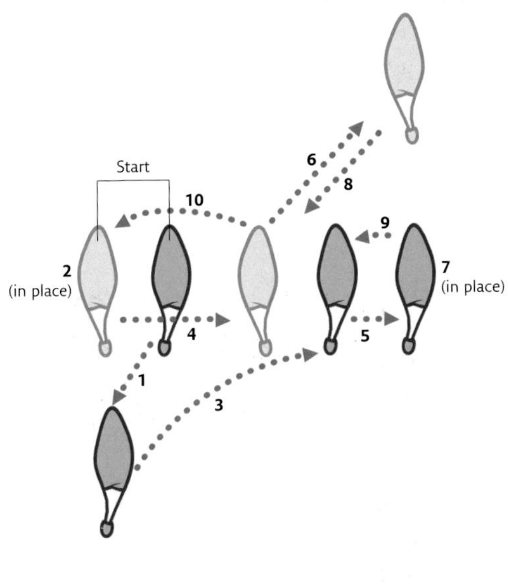

count:

Lady's Steps

step 1 **Right foot** takes a step backwards, taking one beat of music.

step 2 **Left foot** remains in place with the weight taken forwards onto it, taking one beat of music.

cha 3 **Right foot** takes a step to the side, taking half a beat of music.

cha 4 **Left foot** closes towards but not up to right foot, taking half a beat of music.

chah 5 **Right foot** takes a step to the side, taking one beat of music.

step 6 **Left foot** takes a step forwards, taking one beat of music.

step 7 **Right foot** remains in place with the weight taken back onto it, taking one beat of music.

cha 8 **Left foot** takes a step to the side, taking half a beat of music.

cha 9 **Right foot** closes towards but not up to left foot, taking half a beat of music.

chah 10 **Left foot** takes a step to the side, taking one beat of music.

Forwards and Backwards Cha Cha Cha Basics

must know

A non-moving dance
Remember, the Cha Cha Cha does not move around the room and therefore you can face any direction at the start of the figure. However, at first, the man should try facing the nearest wall and the lady should face him. It's a good idea to practise with your hands on your partner's shoulders. You can always hold a chair in front of you if you don't have a partner.

1

count: step

M **Left foot** takes a step forwards.

L **Right foot** takes a step backwards.

Takes one beat of music.

4

count: cha

M **Right foot** closes towards left foot.

L **Left foot** closes towards right foot.

Takes half a beat of music.

2

count: step

M **Right foot** remains in place with the weight back onto it.

L **Left foot** remains in place with the weight taken forwards onto it.

Takes one beat of music.

3

count: cha

M **Left foot** takes a step to the side.

L **Right foot** takes a step to the side.

Takes half a beat of music.

5

count: chah

M **Left foot** takes a step to the side.

L **Right foot** takes a step to the side.

Takes one beat of music.

6

count: step

M **Right foot** takes a step backwards.

L **Left foot** takes a step forwards.

Takes one beat of music.

Forwards and Backwards Cha Cha Cha Basics (continued)

7

count: step

M **Left foot** remains in place with the weight taken forwards onto it.

L **Right foot** remains in place with the weight back onto it.

Takes one beat of music.

8

count: cha

M **Right foot** takes a step to the side.

L **Left foot** takes a step to the side.

Takes half a beat of music.

9

count: cha

M **Left foot** closes towards right foot.

L **Right foot** closes towards left foot.

Takes half a beat of music.

10

count: chah

M **Right foot** takes a step to the side.

L **Left foot** takes a step to the side.

Takes one beat of music.

In Place Basic Cha Cha Chas

This figure is also known as Time Steps. The man and the lady should start with their feet slightly apart – the man facing the wall and the lady with her back to it.

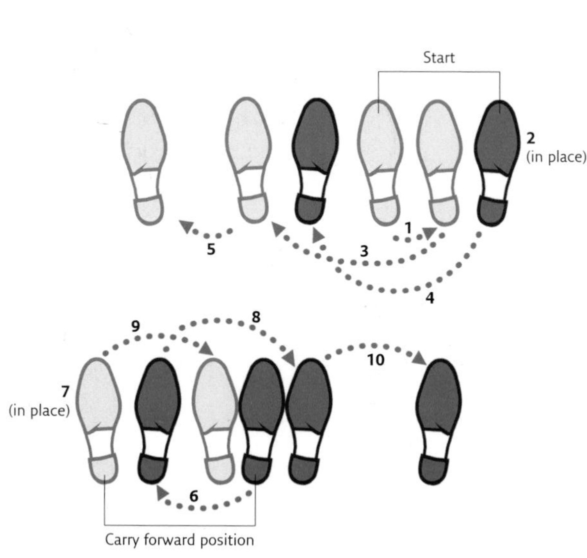

count: **Man's Steps**

step 1 Left foot closes to right foot.

step 2 Right foot marks time in place.

cha 3 Left foot takes a small step to the side, starting the cha cha cha rhythm break leftwards, that is, moving in the opposite direction to the preceding step.

cha 4 Right foot closes towards but not up to left foot.

chah 5 Left foot takes a small step to the side.

step 6 Right foot closes to left foot.

step 7 Left foot marks time in place.

cha 8 Right foot takes a small step to the side, starting the cha cha cha rhythm break rightwards, that is, moving in the opposite direction to the preceding step.

cha 9 Left foot closes towards but not up to right foot.

chah 10 Right foot takes a small step to the side.

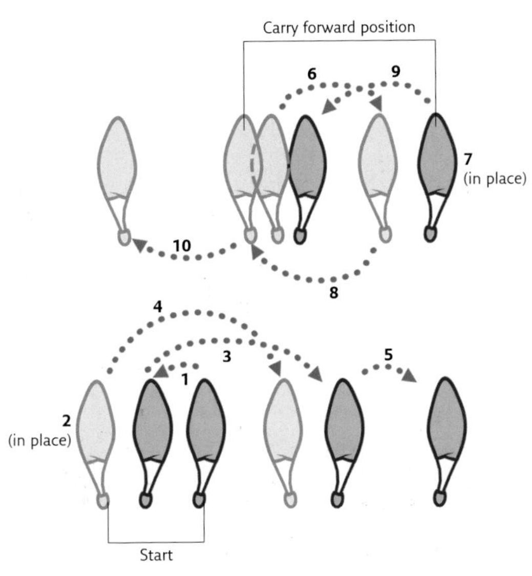

count:

Lady's Steps

step **1** **Right foot** closes to left foot.

step **2** **Left foot** marks time in place.

cha **3** **Right foot** takes a small step to the side, starting the cha cha cha rhythm break rightwards, that is, moving in the opposite direction to the preceding step.

cha **4** **Left foot** closes towards but not up to right foot.

chah **5** **Right foot** takes a small step to the side.

step **6** **Left foot** closes to right foot.

step **7** **Right foot** marks time in place.

cha **8** **Left foot** takes a small step to the side, starting the cha cha cha rhythm break leftwards, that is, moving in opposite direction to preceding step.

cha **9** **Right foot** closes towards but not up to left foot.

chah **10** **Left foot** takes a small step to the side.

In Place Basic Cha Cha Chas

1

count: step

M Left foot closes to right foot.

L Right foot closes to left foot.

2

count: step

M Right foot marks time in place.

L Left foot marks time in place.

3

count: cha

M Left foot to the side, starting the cha cha cha rhythm break leftwards.

L Right foot to the side, starting the cha cha cha rhythm break rightwards.

4

count: cha

M Right foot closes towards but not up to left foot.

L Left foot closes towards but not up to right foot.

(continued overleaf)

In Place Basic Cha Cha Chas (continued)

5

count: chah

M **Left foot** takes a small step to the side.

L **Right foot** takes a small step to the side.

6

count: step

M **Right foot** closes to left foot.

L **Left foot** closes to right foot.

8

count: cha

M **Right foot** to the side, starting the cha cha cha rhythm break rightwards.

L **Left foot** to the side, starting the cha cha cha rhythm break leftwards.

9

count: cha

M **Left foot** closes towards but not up to right foot.

L **Right foot** closes towards but not up to left foot.

7

count: step

M Left foot marks time in place.

L Right foot marks time in place.

10

count: chah

M Right foot takes a small step to the side.

L Left foot takes a small step to the side.

must know

Footwork

When you are dancing the Cha Cha Cha think about your footwork. Step onto the ball of your foot first and then lower your heel. On the cha cha chah rhythm take small steps, making sure that the move is in time with the music.

The Fan

In the Fan, the man releases hold of the lady with his right hand, guides her to move to his left side and turn, so that she is facing him at roughly right angles.

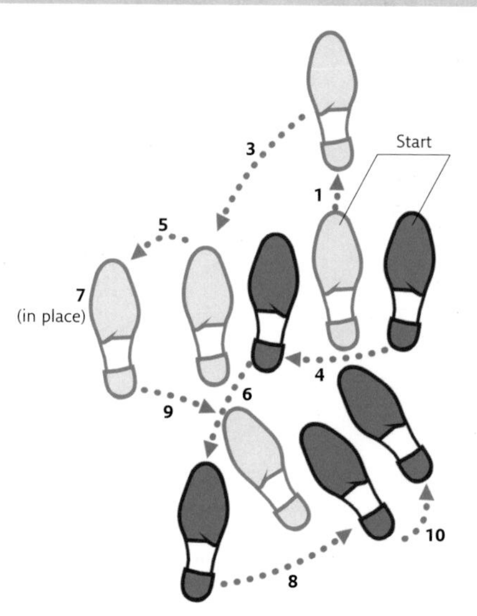

count: **Man's Steps**

step **1** **Left foot** takes a small step forwards.

step **2** **Right foot** remains in place with the weight back onto it.

cha **3** **Left foot** takes a step to the side, turning to the left.

cha **4** **Right foot** closes towards but not up to left foot.

chah **5** **Left foot** takes a step to the side, turning to the left and lowering your left arm.

step **6** **Right foot** takes a step backwards, leading partner to step to the left of your feet, that is, 'outside partner'.

step **7** **Left foot** remains in place with the weight taken forwards onto it. Turn the lady to her left by pulling your left hand back and releasing hold of her with your right hand.

cha **8** **Right foot** takes a step to the side, turning to your left. The lady should almost be at right angles to you and stepping back away from you.

cha **9** **Left foot** closes towards right foot, still turning to your left.

chah **10** **Right foot** takes a small step to the side. You are now at right angles to your partner, holding her right hand in your left hand.

must know

At the end of this figure you will end up in what dancers call the Fan position. The Fan is usually followed by the Hockey Stick (see pages 94–9).

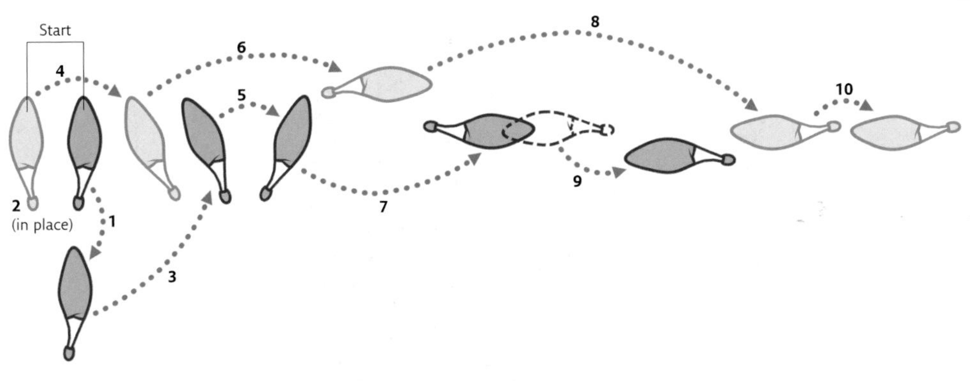

Lady's Steps

count:

count		
step	1	**Right foot** takes a small step backwards.
step	2	**Left foot** remains in place with the weight forwards onto it.
cha	3	**Right foot** takes a step to the side turning to the left.
cha	4	**Left foot** closes towards but not up to right foot.
chah	5	**Right foot** takes a step to the side, turning to the right and lowering your right arm.
step	6	**Left foot** takes a step forwards to your right of both your partner's feet, that is, 'outside partner'.
step	7	**Right foot** takes a step forwards, then turn to the left on both feet to finish with your right foot backwards.
cha	8	**Left foot** takes a step backwards, still turning to the left to finish at almost right angles to your partner.
cha	9	**Right foot** closes towards left foot, still turning to the left. At this point you can cross the right foot in front of the left foot.
chah	10	**Left foot** takes a small step backwards. You are now at right angles to your partner, he is holding your right hand in his left hand.

The Fan

must know

Listen to the music

It is said that the name Cha Cha Cha comes from the sound of the dancers' feet as they scraped across the floor to the cha cha cha triple beat rhythm. If you listen it is not hard to hear. First count each bar of music, 'one, two, three, four'; the count of 'four' takes two steps, which we have counted 'Cha Cha' and each takes half a beat of music. The first step of the next bar takes one beat of music, which we have we counted 'Chah'.

1

count: step

M Left foot takes a small step forwards.

L Right foot takes a small step backwards.

4

count: cha

M Right foot closes towards but not up to left foot.

L Left foot closes towards but not up to right foot.

2

count: step

M Right foot remains in place taking the weight back onto it.

L Left foot remains in place with the weight forwards onto it.

3

count: cha

M Left foot takes a step to the side, turning to the left.

L Right foot takes a step to the side turning to the left.

5

count: chah

M Left foot to the side, turning to the left and lowering left arm.

L Right foot to the side, turning to the right and lowering right arm.

6

count: step

M Right foot takes a step backwards, leading partner to step 'outside partner'.

L Left foot takes a step forwards, 'outside partner'.

(continued overleaf)

The Fan (continued)

7

count: step

M Left foot remains forwards in place. Turn lady to left, release hold of her with right hand.

L Right foot forwards, then turn to left, end with right foot backwards.

9

count: cha

M Left foot closes towards right foot.

L Right foot closes towards left foot, still turning to the left. You can cross the right foot in front of the left foot.

8
count: cha

M **Right foot** takes a step to the side.

L **Left foot** takes a step backwards, still turning to the left, now almost at right angles to your partner.

10
count: chah

M **Right foot** takes a step to the side.

L **Left foot** takes a step backwards. You are now at right angles to your partner.

did you know?

Tea for two
Early British recordings of Cha Cha Cha music that you may have heard are: 'Cherry Blossom Pink and Apple Blossom White' and 'Tea for Two Cha Cha'. These popular tunes helped to establish the dance. In 1962 the Cha Cha Cha was accepted by the British Dance Council for its championships.

The Hockey Stick

In this figure, which follows the Fan (see pages 88–93), the man turns the lady to her left under his left and her right hands. Partners will end up facing each other.

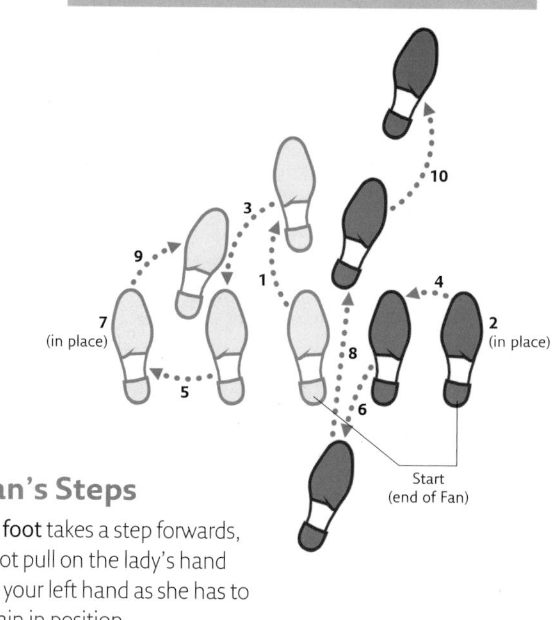

count:

Man's Steps

step 1 **Left foot** takes a step forwards, do not pull on the lady's hand with your left hand as she has to remain in position.

step 2 **Right foot** remains in place with the weight back onto it, starting to bring your left hand forwards and across your body, guiding the lady forwards.

cha 3 **Left foot** takes a step to the side, starting to raise your left hand.

cha 4 **Right foot** closes towards but not up to left foot, keeping left hand raised.

chah 5 **Left foot** takes a step to the side, passing your left and the lady's right hand over the lady's head, then lower your left hand onto her shoulder. Do not grip her hand tightly, she must be free to turn.

step 6 **Right foot** takes a step backwards, starting to turn a little to the right.

step 7 **Left foot** remains in place with the weight forwards onto it, then lower your left hand to the normal position. By the end of the step the lady will be facing you.

cha 8 **Right foot** takes a step forwards towards partner.

cha 9 **Left foot** closes towards right foot.

chah 10 **Right foot** takes a step forwards.

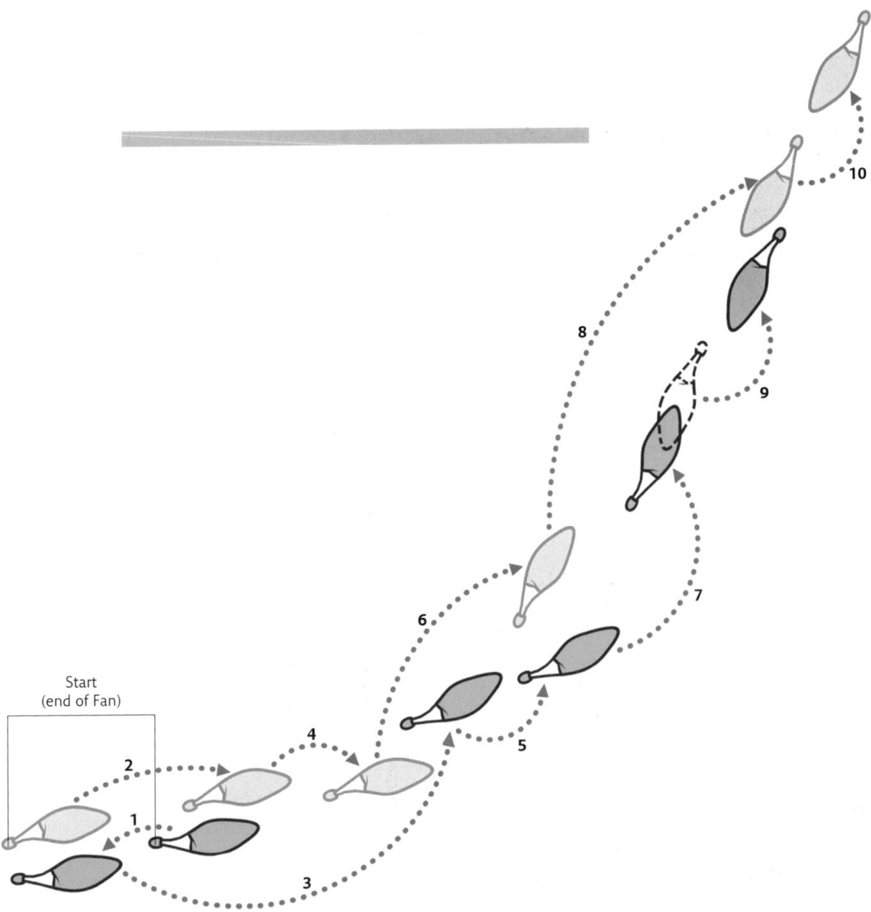

count:

Lady's Steps

step 1 Right foot closes towards left foot.

step 2 Left foot takes a step forwards, moving towards partner.

cha 3 Right foot takes a step forwards.

cha 4 Left foot closes towards right foot, or, if you are adventurous, loosely cross it behind your right foot.

chah 5 Right foot takes a step forwards, moving your right hand over your head onto your left shoulder.

step 6 Left foot takes a step forwards, starting to turn left.

step 7 Right foot steps forwards, then turn to the left on both feet to finish with right foot backwards, facing partner.

cha 8 Left foot takes a step backwards.

cha 9 Right foot closes towards left foot.

chah 10 Left foot takes a step backwards, facing your partner with your right hand in his left hand and with your left hand free.

The Hockey Stick

must know

The Lock Step
In the Cha Cha Chah rhythmic break (see page 74), advanced dancers use a lock step (step, cross, step) when moving either forwards or backwards.
For example, a forwards lock step is:
1 Right foot forwards.
2 Left foot crosses loosely behind right foot.
3 Right foot forwards.
When you are moving backwards, the second step crosses loosely in front of the first step backwards.

1
count: step

M Left foot forwards, do not pull on the lady's hand as she has to remain in position.

L Right foot closes towards left foot.

3
count: cha

M Left foot takes a step to the side, starting to raise your left hand.

L Right foot takes a step forwards.

2

count: step

M **Right foot** remains in place with weight back onto it, starting to guide the lady to step forwards.

L **Left foot** takes a step forwards, moving towards partner.

4

count: cha

M **Right foot** closes towards left foot, keeping left hand raised.

L **Left foot** closes towards right foot, you can loosely cross it behind your right foot.

(continued overleaf)

The Hockey Stick (continued)

5

count: chah

M Left foot to the side, passing your left and lady's right hands over her head, lowering hands onto her left shoulder.

L Right foot takes a step forwards.

6

count: step

M Right foot steps backwards, starting to turn a little to the right.

L Left foot steps forwards, starting to turn to the left.

8

count: cha

M Right foot takes a step forwards towards partner.

L Left foot takes a step backwards.

9

count: cha

M Left foot closes towards right foot.

L Right foot closes towards left foot.

7

count: step

M Left foot remains forwards in place, then lower left hand to normal position.

L Right foot forwards, then turn to left to finish facing partner.

10

count: chah

M Right foot takes a step forwards.

L Left foot takes a step backwards.

must know

Back to normal

At the end of the Hockey Stick, partners are still separated and have not returned to the normal hold. This is achieved by the man drawing the lady towards him while dancing the basic movement.

The Alemana

In this figure the lady turns to her right instead of her left. The instructions below are for the Alemana taken from the Fan position (see page 89).

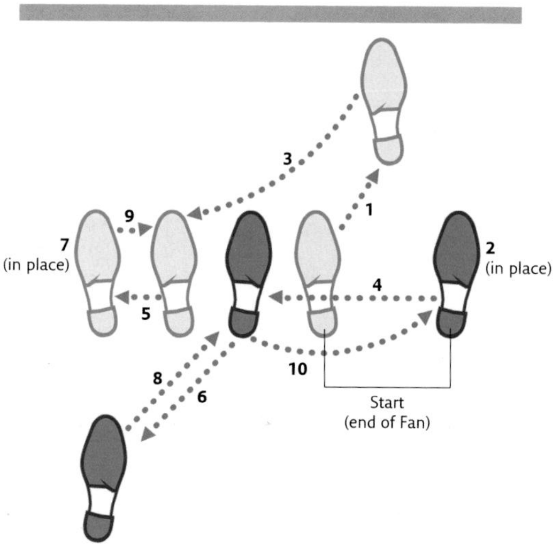

count:

Man's Steps

The man does not turn in this figure.

step 1 Left foot takes a small step forwards, do not pull on the lady's hand with your left hand as she has to remain momentarily away from you.

step 2 Right foot remains in place with the weight back onto it, starting to bring your left hand forwards and across your body, guiding partner forwards.

cha 3 Left foot takes a step to the side, starting to raise your left hand.

cha 4 Right foot closes towards but not up to left foot, keeping left hand raised.

chah 5 Left foot takes a step to the side, starting to turn the lady strongly to her right by rotating the joined hands clockwise. Do not grip tightly.

step 6 Right foot takes a step backwards, continuing to turn partner to her right.

step 7 Left foot remains in place with the weight forwards onto it, continuing to turn the lady to her right.

cha 8 Right foot takes a step to the side, with the lady still turning.

cha 9 Left foot closes towards right foot, with the lady still turning.

chah 10 Right foot takes a step to the side, you are now facing your partner. Regain normal hold.

must know

After the Fan, rather than the Hockey Stick, the Alemana can be danced.

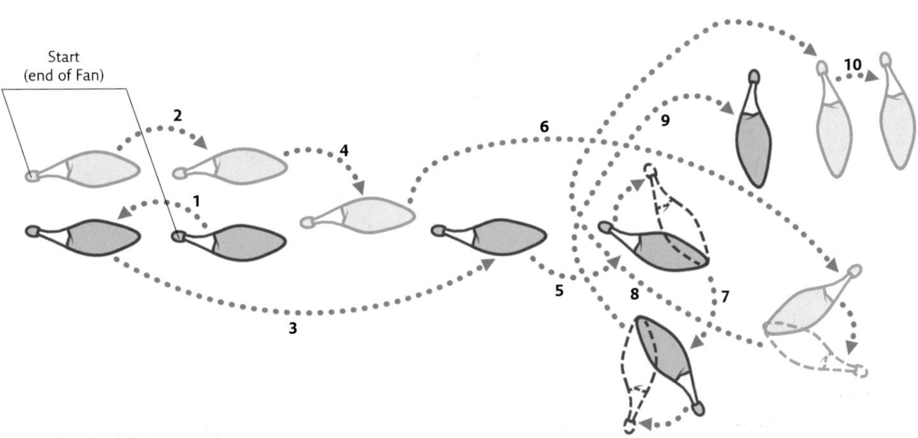

count:

Lady's Steps

In steps 5–10 imagine you are walking around a small plate, you will make one and a quarter turns to your right.

step 1 **Right foot** closes to left foot.

step 2 **Left foot** takes a step forwards moving towards partner.

cha 3 **Right foot** takes a step forwards.

cha 4 **Left foot** closes towards right foot, and can cross loosely behind it.

chah 5 **Right foot** takes a step forwards, starting the strong turn to the right.

step 6 **Left foot** takes a step forwards, turning strongly to the right.

step 7 **Right foot** takes a step forwards, still turning strongly to the right.

cha 8 **Left foot** takes a step to the side, still turning to the right.

cha 9 **Right foot** closes towards left foot, still turning to the right.

chah 10 **Left foot** takes a step to the side, you are now facing your partner. Regain normal hold.

The Alemana

watch out!

On figures where the man has to turn the lady under an arch formed by his left and her right hand, the man must be careful to guide his partner and not to fall into the trap of being too forceful as if he had provided the power for her to make her turn. The same caution applies to any figure where the man is guiding the turn by use of hands alone.

1

count: step

M Left foot takes a step forwards, do not pull on the lady's hand, she has to remain in position.

L Right foot closes to left foot.

3

count: cha

M Left foot takes a step to the side, starting to raise your left hand.

L Right foot takes a step forwards.

2

count: step

M **Right foot** remains in place with weight back onto it, while left hand guides partner forwards.

L **Left foot** takes a step forwards, moving towards partner.

4

count: cha

M **Right foot** closes towards but not up to left foot, keeping your left hand raised.

L **Left foot** closes towards right foot and may cross behind it.

The Alemana (continued)

5

count: chah

M Left foot takes a step to the side, starting to turn the lady strongly to her right.

L Right foot takes a step forwards, starting the strong turn to the right.

6

count: step

M Right foot takes a step backwards, still turning partner to her right.

L Left foot takes a step forwards, turning strongly to the right.

8

count: cha

M Right foot takes a step to the side, lady still turning.

L Left foot takes a step to the side, still turning to the right.

9

count: cha

M Left foot closes towards right foot, with the lady still turning.

L Right foot closes towards left foot, still turning to the right.

7

count: step

M Left foot remains in place with the weight forwards onto it, still turning lady to her right.

L Right foot takes a step forwards, still turning strongly to the right.

10

count: chah

M Right foot takes a step to the side to face your partner. Regain normal hold.

L Left foot takes a step to the side to face your partner. Regain normal hold.

want to know more?

- Revise the basic movements until you feel confident with the steps, then broaden your repertoire.
- Try the figures at different music speeds.
- Make sure you can dance the figures in rooms of any size or shape.
- Join a dance school. For addresses look in local newspapers, Yellow Pages and see pages 184–9.
- Check with your local authority for evening classes.

weblinks

- Consult the websites of the dance teachers' organizations listed on pages 184–5.
- For information on dance competitions: www.dancesport.uk
- For books, CDs, DVDs: www.dancebooks.co.uk
- For videos, visit www.activevideos.com

5 Salsa

The essence of Salsa is the turning of the man and lady with respect to each other, often under joined arms that have formed an arch. A fascinating mix of Cuban and North American dance styles and rhythms, it has evidence of both cultures and a vitality all of its own. In Salsa figures, because of the numerous turns, both partners have to make more use of the hands and arms than in many other dances, and need to pay particular care and attention to their use.

A cocktail of rhythm

Today, Salsa is probably the most popular of the Cuban-based dances and, musically, it is a complicated blend of Cuban dance forms such as Son, Danson, Guarjira, Mambo and Cha Cha Cha.

To this cocktail of rhythm has been added the drive and vitality of the American music scene with its jazz and rock traditions. A very heady mixture full of life and vitality is the result.

The Spanish word salsa means sauce, but musicians think of it more as spice and this is just what you should have in mind when attempting the dance. The music first came to notice in the 1960s in the USA, and perhaps the confirmation that it had arrived was the release of the film *Salsa* in 1988.

A demonstration of this energetic dance by members of the Eddie Torres Salsa Company.

Body action

This is a dance where body action is as important as movement, if not more so. The dances from Latin-America, and particularly those from the Caribbean, are complex with historical influences from the original natives, the Spanish invaders and the multitude of African slaves that were imported into the countries. From the African slaves came the complex drum and rhythm instrument patterns, and also the erect carriage of the body that was essential for anyone who had to carry containers on their head. Stemming from this custom, the shoulders and head are kept still, so far as possible, in the steps of dances with a Caribbean history such as Salsa.

The hold and hip action

For this dance use the Open Hold (see pages 14–15). Movement of the hips is common to many Latin dances with a Cuban/Caribbean history. It is described in some detail below. Much of the enjoyment and, indeed, the exercise benefits of these dances comes from a fluid hip action.

Start with your feet a few inches apart and knees relaxed. Take the weight fully onto your flat left foot, straightening the knee and letting the weight of your body settle onto your left hip, pushing it out sideways. If you have a fluid waist this will be easy, if not, this will assist you in achieving one. Now take the weight over the flat right foot. Straighten the right knee letting the weight of your body settle onto the right hip, pushing it out sideways. This settling of the weight over the supporting foot allows the hips to move sideways, and takes place on most steps where weight is transferred onto the foot. However, on a step that has two beats of music, the settling of the hip takes place on the second beat.

did you know?

Taking a turn

The turns in Salsa can be very intricate. If you are fortunate enough to be practising with a partner, try the Man and Lady Twirls (see pages 132–5), which consists of a fairly simple group of turning steps. Some couples find it easier to make the turns if the man bends his second finger of his left hand down from the remaining fingers and the lady loosely holds the finger and uses it as a pivot for the turns.

The Left Side Basic

Once you have practised these steps on your own, you should try to master them with a partner. With a partner, when the man dances the Left Side Basic the lady dances the man's Right Side Basic (see pages 112–13) and vice versa. This figure can follow the Right Side Basic and vice versa, making a pattern of eight steps that can be repeated as often as you wish. Each step takes one beat of music.

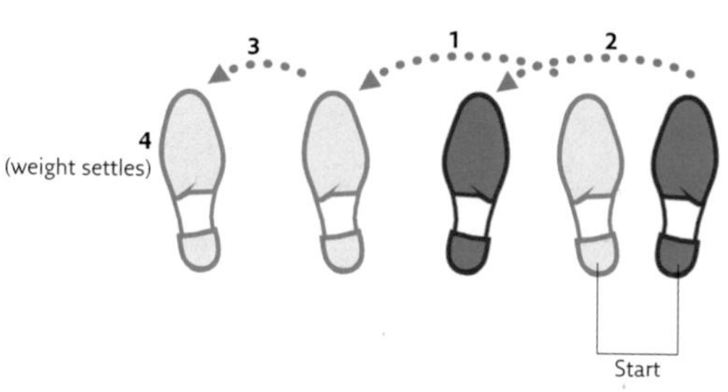

count: **Man's Steps**

one 1 Left foot takes a small step to the side, straighten the leg and settle weight onto the foot so that your hips swing over to the left.

two 2 Right foot closes half way towards left foot, straighten the leg and settle weight onto the foot so that hips swing over to right.

three 3 Left foot takes a small step to the side, keeping the leg relaxed, without putting your full weight onto the foot.

four 4 Left leg straightens and weight is settled fully over the foot so that hips swing over to the left and, at the same time, tap the toes of your right foot to the side of your left foot.

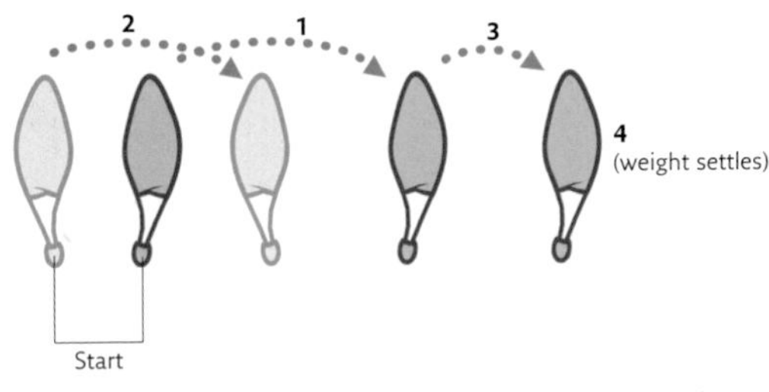

count:

Lady's Steps

one 1 Right foot takes a small step to the side, straighten the leg and settle weight onto the foot so that your hips swing over to the right.

two 2 Left foot closes half way towards right foot, straighten the leg and settle weight onto the foot so that hips swing over to the left.

three 3 Right foot takes a small step to the side, keeping the leg relaxed, without putting your full weight onto the foot.

four 4 Right leg straightens and weight is settled fully over the foot so that hips swing over to the right and, at the same time, tap the toes of your left foot to the side of your right foot.

The Right Side Basic

The Right Side Basic can follow the Left Side Basic (see pages 110–11) and vice versa, making a pattern of eight steps that can be repeated as often as you wish.

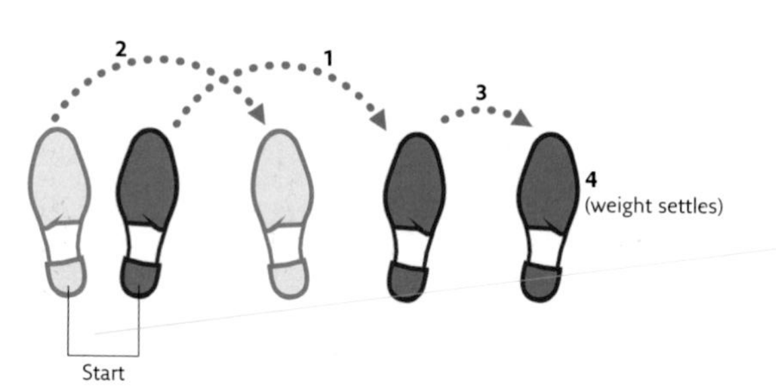

count: **Man's Steps**

one 1 **Right foot** takes a small step to the side, straighten the leg and settle weight onto the foot so that your hips swing over to the right.

two 2 **Left foot** closes half way towards right foot, straighten the leg and settle weight onto the foot so that hips swing over to the left.

three 3 **Right foot** takes a small step to the side, keeping the leg relaxed and without putting your full weight onto the foot.

four 4 **Right leg** straightens and weight is settled fully over the foot so that hips swing over to the right and, at the same time, tap the toes of your left foot to the side of your right foot.

did you know?

A developing dance
Salsa is danced to music that is Cuban in origin but which has been massively influenced by American jazz. Some dances remain more or less the same for many years. The Salsa, however, is still developing, but this will not affect the basic figures described here.

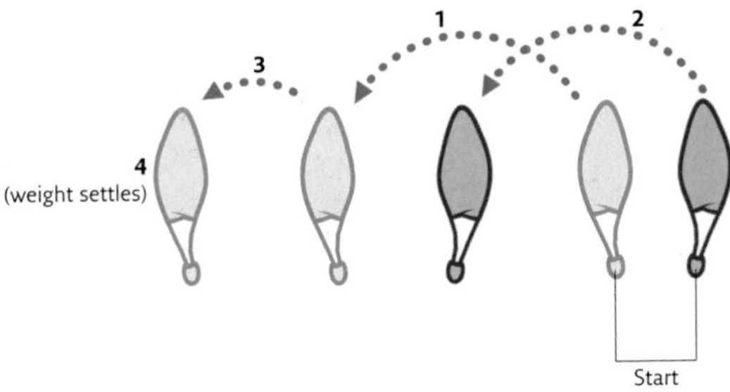

count:

Lady's Steps

one 1 **Left foot** takes a small step to the side, straighten the leg and settle weight onto the foot so that your hips swing over to the left.

two 2 **Right foot** closes half way towards left foot, straighten the leg and settle weight onto the foot so that hips swing over to right.

three 3 **Left foot** takes a small step to the side, keeping the leg relaxed, and without putting your full weight onto the foot.

four 4 **Left leg** straightens and weight is settled fully over the foot so that hips swing over to the left and, at the same time, tap the toes of your right foot to the side of your left foot.

The Left Side Basic

1

count: one

M **Left foot** to side, leg straightens, weight on foot, swing hips to left.

L **Right foot** to side, leg straightens, weight on foot, swing hips to right.

2

count: two

M **Right foot** closes towards left foot, swing hips to the right.

L **Left foot** closes towards right foot, leg straightens, swing hips to the left.

3

count: three

M **Left foot** to the side, without putting full weight onto the foot.

L **Right foot** to the side, without putting full weight onto the foot.

4

count: four

M **Left leg** straightens, swing hips to the left and tap right toes.

L **Right leg** straightens, swing hips to the right and tap left toes.

The Right Side Basic

1

count: one

M **Right foot** to side, leg straightens, weight on foot, swing hips to right.

L **Left foot** to side, leg straightens, weight on foot, swing hips to left.

2

count: two

M **Left foot** closes towards right foot, swing hips to the left.

L **Right foot** closes towards left foot, leg straightens, swing hips to the right.

3

count: three

M **Right foot** to the side, without putting full weight onto the foot.

L **Left foot** to the side, without putting full weight onto the foot.

4

count: four

M **Right leg** straightens, swing hips to the right and tap left toes.

L **Left leg** straightens, swing hips to the left and tap right toes.

Cucaracha Steps

One of the earliest Latin 'dances' to achieve real popularity was the Cucaracha (Spanish for cockroach). A dance with that name was featured in the Fred Astaire–Ginger Rogers film, *Flying Down to Rio*. How the name has come to be associated with this figure is not clear but it is a typical basic movement in Salsa and can also be found in some other Latin dances. In the following instructions each step takes one beat of music.

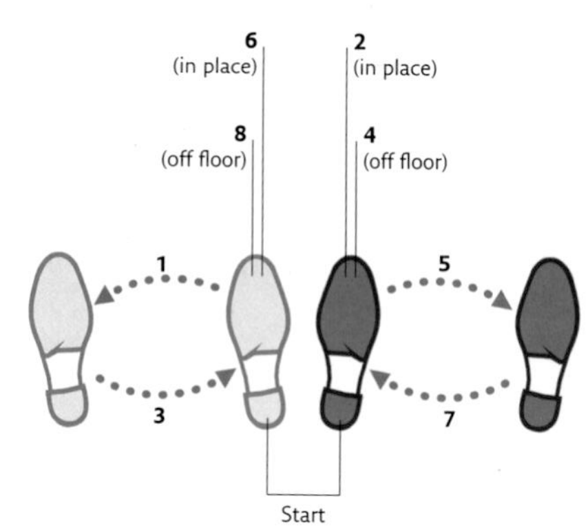

count:

Man's Steps

one 1 Left foot takes a step to the side, pressing downwards into the floor but still retain some pressure on the right foot, while allowing the hips to swing to the left.

two 2 Left foot pushes off against the floor, taking the weight back fully onto the right foot, straighten right knee and allow the hips to swing to the right.

three 3 Left foot closes to right foot taking the weight onto left foot.

four 4 Right foot lifts just off the floor with a flick action.

one 5 Right foot takes a step to the side, pressing downwards into the floor but still retain some pressure on the left foot, while allowing the hips to swing to right.

two 6 Right foot pushes off against the floor, taking the weight back fully onto the left foot, straighten left knee and allow the hips to swing to the left.

three 7 Right foot closes to left foot, taking the weight onto right foot.

four 8 Left foot lifts just off the floor with a flick action.

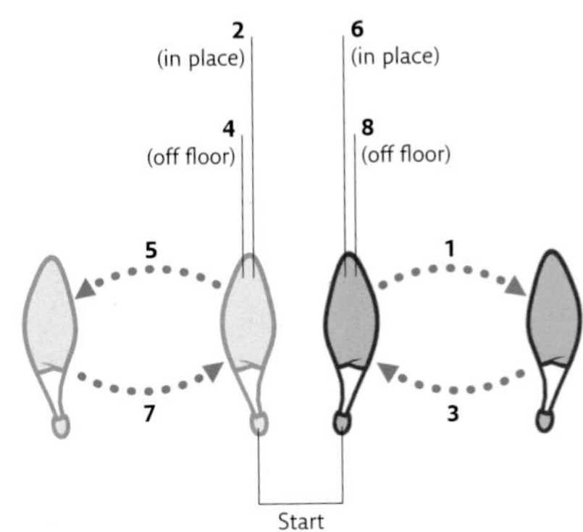

count:

Lady's Steps

one 1 Right foot takes a step to the side, pressing downwards into the floor but still retain some pressure on the left foot, while allowing the hips to swing to right.

two 2 Right foot pushes off against the floor, taking the weight back fully onto the left foot, straighten left knee and allow the hips to swing to the left.

three 3 Right foot closes to left foot taking the weight onto right foot.

four 4 Left foot lifts just off the floor with a flick action.

one 5 Left foot takes a step to the side, pressing downwards into the floor but still retain some pressure on the right foot, while allowing the hips to swing to left.

two 6 Left foot pushes off against the floor, taking weight back fully onto the right foot, straighten right knee and allow the hips to swing to the right.

three 7 Left foot closes to right foot, taking the weight onto left foot.

four 8 Right foot lifts just off the floor with a flick action.

Cucaracha Steps

1

count: one

M **Left foot** to the side, retain pressure on right foot, swing hips to left.

L **Right foot** to the side, retain some pressure on left foot, swing hips to right.

2

count: two

M **Left foot** pushes off against the floor, weight onto right foot, swing hips to right.

L **Right foot** pushes off against the floor, weight onto left foot, hips to left.

5

count: one

M **Right foot** to the side, retain pressure on left foot, swing hips to right.

L **Left foot** to the side, retain pressure on right foot, swing hips to left.

6

count: two

M **Right foot** pushes off against the floor, weight onto left foot, hips to left.

L **Left foot** pushes off against floor, weight onto right foot, swing hips to right.

3

count: three

M **Left foot** closes to right foot, taking the weight onto left foot.

L **Right foot** closes to left foot, taking the weight onto right foot.

4

count: four

M **Right foot** lifts just off the floor with a flick action.

L **Left foot** lifts just off the floor with a flick action.

7

count: three

M **Right foot** closes to left foot, taking the weight onto right foot.

L **Left foot** closes to right foot, taking the weight onto left foot.

8

count: four

M **Left foot** lifts just off the floor with a flick action.

L **Right foot** lifts just off the floor with a flick action.

Forwards and Backwards Basics

This figure can be danced after the Right Side Basic (see pages 112–15) or the Cucaracha Steps (see pages 116–19). Each step takes one beat of music.

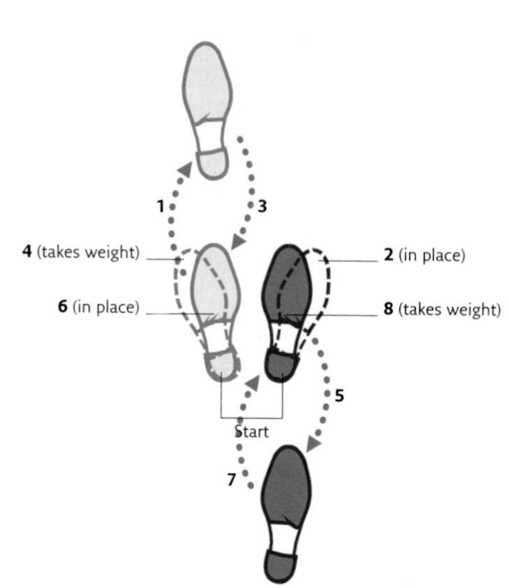

count: **Man's Steps**

one **1** **Left foot** left foot takes a step forwards, settling hips to the left as the weight is taken onto the foot.

two **2** **Right foot** remains in place, settling hips to the right as the weight is taken backwards onto the foot.

three **3** **Left foot** closes to right foot with light pressure on the floor.

four **4** **Left foot** takes the weight, at the same time, lift the right heel just off the floor.

one **5** **Right foot** takes a step backwards, settling hips to the right as the weight is taken onto the foot.

two **6** **Left foot** remains in place, settling hips to the left as the weight is taken forwards onto the foot.

three **7** **Right foot** closes to left foot with light pressure on the floor.

four **8** **Right foot** takes the full weight, at same time, lift the left heel just off the floor.

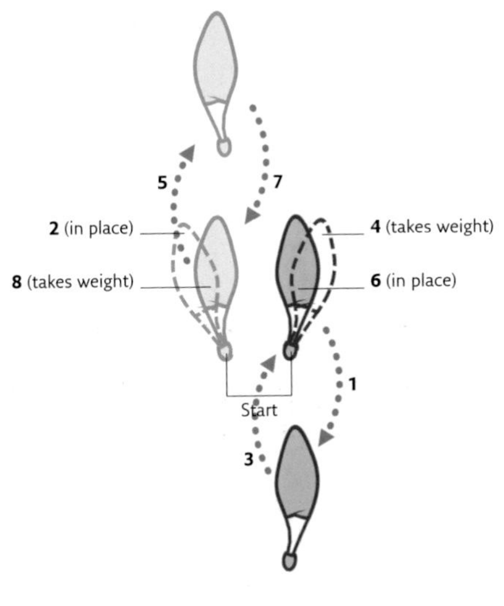

count: **Lady's Steps**

one 1 Right foot takes a step backwards, settling hips to the right as the weight is taken onto the foot.

two 2 Left foot remains in place, settling hips to the left as the weight is taken forwards onto the foot.

three 3 Right foot closes to left foot with light pressure on the floor.

four 4 Right foot takes the weight, at the same time, lift the left heel just off the floor.

one 5 Left foot takes a step forwards, settling hips to the left as the weight is taken onto the foot.

two 6 Right foot remains in place, settling hips to the right as the weight is taken backwards onto the foot.

three 7 Left foot closes to right foot with light pressure on the floor.

four 8 Left foot takes the full weight, at same time, lift the right heel just off the floor.

Forwards and Backwards Basics

1

count: one

M Left foot forwards, hips to the left as weight is taken onto the foot.

L Right foot backwards, hips to the right as weight is taken onto the foot.

2

count: two

M Right foot remains in place, takes the weight onto it, hips to the right.

L Left foot remains in place, takes the weight onto it, hips to the left.

5

count: one

M Right foot backwards, hips to the right as weight is taken onto the foot.

L Left foot forwards, hips to the left as weight is taken onto the foot.

6

count: two

M Left foot remains in place, takes the weight onto it, hips to the left.

L Right foot remains in place, takes the weight onto it, hips to the right.

3

count: three

M **Left foot** closes to right foot with light pressure on the floor.

L **Right foot** closes to left foot with light pressure on the floor.

4

count: four

M **Left foot** takes the weight onto it, lift the right heel just off the floor.

L **Right foot** takes the weight onto it, lift the left heel just off the floor.

7

count: three

M **Right foot** closes to left foot with light pressure on the floor.

L **Left foot** closes to right foot with light pressure on the floor.

8

count: four

M **Right foot** takes the weight onto it, lift the left heel just off the floor.

L **Left foot** takes the weight onto it, lift the right heel just off the floor.

Left and Right Breaks

This group can follow the Right Side Basic (see pages 112–13), Cucaracha Steps (see pages 116–19), and Forwards and Backwards Basics (see pages 120–3).

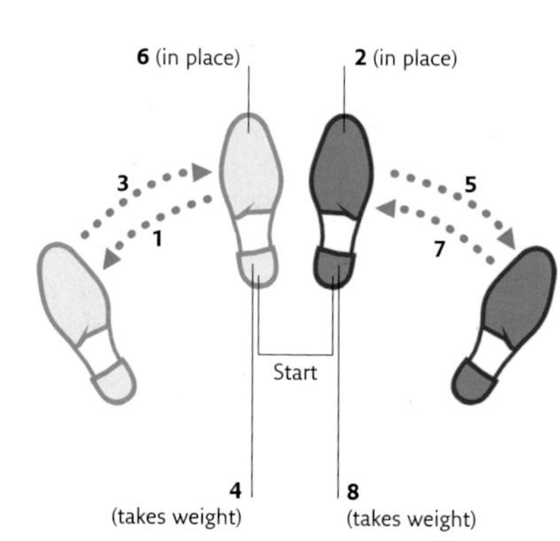

count: **Man's Steps**

one 1 Left foot takes a small step to the side, turn a little to the left, lower your left hand and push the lady's hand back slightly causing her to turn to her right.

two 2 Right foot remains in place but the weight is taken forwards onto it. Pull your left hand back a little, leading the lady to face you.

three 3 Left foot closes to right foot with light pressure on the floor.

four 4 Left foot takes the weight onto it, at the same time, lift the right heel just off the floor.

one 5 Right foot takes a small step to the side, turn a little to the right and push on the lady's side with your right hand so as to guide her to turn to her left and then release hold with your right hand.

two 6 Left foot remains in place but the weight is taken forwards onto it, leading the lady to face you.

three 7 Right foot closes to left foot with light pressure on the floor, turning to the left, guiding the lady to face you and regaining hold of her with your right hand.

four 8 Right foot takes the weight onto it, at the same time, lift the left heel just off the floor.

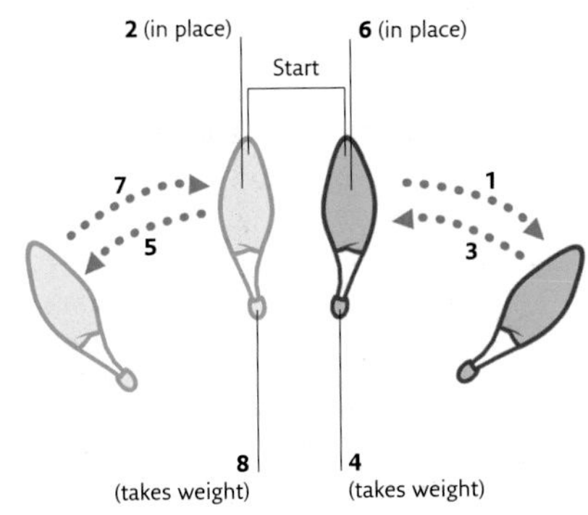

count:

Lady's Steps

one **1** **Right foot** takes a small step to the side, lower your right hand and turn a little to the right, as a result of pressure on your hand from your partner.

two **2** **Left foot** remains in place but the weight is taken forwards onto it, turning left to face your partner.

three **3** **Right foot** closes to left foot with light pressure on the floor.

four **4** **Right foot** takes the weight onto it, at the same time, lift the left heel just off the floor.

one **5** **Left foot** takes a small step to the side, turning left and causing the left side your of body to move away from your partner.

two **6** **Right foot** remains in place but weight is taken forwards onto it, turning to your right to face your partner.

three **7** **Left foot** closes to right foot with light pressure on the floor, now facing your partner.

four **8** **Left foot** takes the weight onto it, at the same time, lift the right heel just off the floor.

Left and Right Breaks

1

count: one

M Left foot to side, turn left, push the lady's hand back slightly causing her to turn to her right.

L Right foot to side, lower right hand and turn a little to the right.

2

count: two

M Right foot remains in place but weight is taken forwards onto it.

L Left foot remains in place but weight is taken onto it, turning left to face partner.

5

count: one

M Right foot to side, turn to the right, guide the lady to turn left and let go with your right hand.

L Left foot to the side, turning left and moving away from your partner.

6

count: two

M Left foot remains in place but weight is taken forwards onto it.

L Right foot remains in place but weight is taken onto it, turning right to face your partner.

3

count: three

M **Left foot** closes to right foot with light pressure on the floor.

L **Right foot** closes to left foot with light pressure on the floor.

4

count: four

M **Left foot** takes the weight onto it, at the same time, lift the right heel just off the floor.

L **Right foot** takes the weight onto it, lift the left heel just off the floor.

7

count: three

M **Right foot** closes to left foot, turning left and guiding lady with right hand to face you.

L **Left foot** closes to right foot, now facing your partner.

8

count: four

M **Right foot** takes the weight onto it and lift the left heel just off the floor.

L **Left foot** takes the weight back onto it and lift the right heel just off the floor.

Outside Breaks

This figure follows Cucaracha Steps or Forwards and Backwards Basics (see pages 116–23). It can be repeated and benefits from doing so. When you are comfortable with this figure you might care to try to increase the lady's turns.

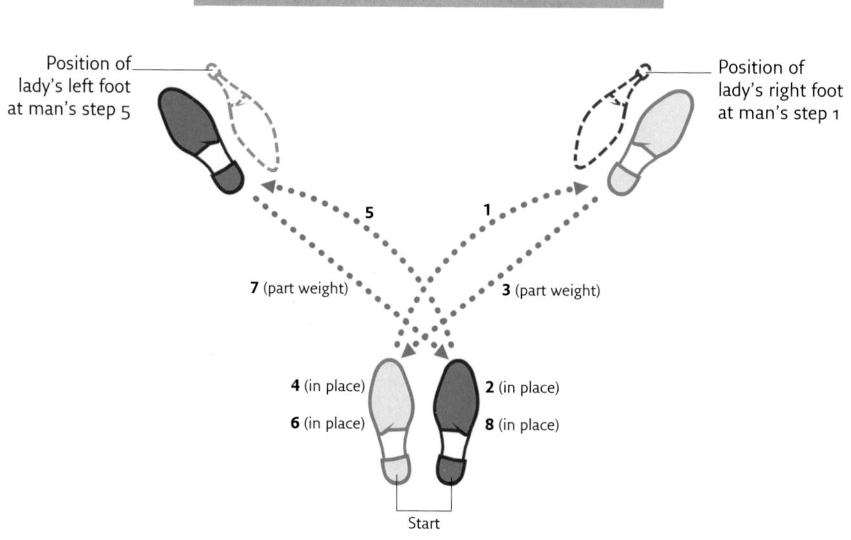

count: **Man's Steps**

one **1** **Left foot** takes a small step forwards and across the body, turning to the right about 45–90 degrees as you step to your right of the lady's feet.

two **2** **Right foot** remains in place and weight is taken backwards onto it, starting to turn to the left.

three **3** **Left foot** to the side of right foot, putting only part weight on foot, completing the turn to the left so as to face your partner again.

four **4** **Left foot** remains in place and weight is taken fully onto it.

one **5** **Right foot** takes a small step forwards and across the body, turning to the left about 45–90 degrees as you step to your left of the lady's feet.

two **6** **Left foot** remains in place and weight is taken backwards onto it, starting to turn to the right.

three **7** **Right foot** to the side of left foot, putting only part weight on foot, completing the turn to the right to face partner again.

four **8** **Right foot** remains in place and weight taken fully onto it.

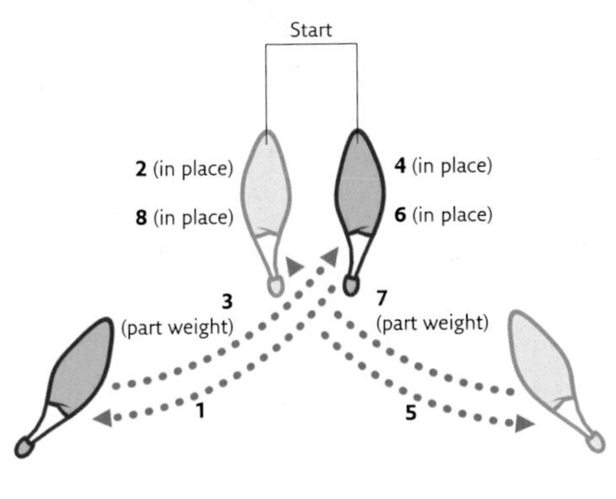

Lady's Steps

count:

one 1 Right foot takes a small step backwards, turning to the right about 45–90 degrees, allowing the man to step to your left side.

two 2 Left foot remains in place and weight is transferred forwards onto it, starting to turn to the left.

three 3 Right foot to the side of left foot, putting only part weight onto foot, completing the turn to the left so as to face your partner again.

four 4 Right foot remains in place and weight is taken fully onto it.

one 5 Left foot takes a small step backwards, turning to the left about 45–90 degrees, allowing the man to step to your right side.

two 6 Right foot remains in place and weight is taken forwards onto it, starting to turn to the right.

three 7 Left foot to the side of right foot, putting only part weight on foot, completing the turn to the right to face partner again.

four 8 Left foot remains in place and weight taken fully onto it.

Outside Breaks

1

count: one

M Left foot forwards, turning right as you step 'outside partner'.

L Right foot backwards, turning right, allowing the man to step to your left side.

2

count: two

M Right foot remains in place, weight is taken onto it, turning left.

L Left foot remains in place and weight is taken onto it, turning to the left.

5

count: one

M Right foot forwards and across the body, turning left as you step 'outside partner'.

L Left foot backwards, turning to the left, as man steps to your right.

6

count: two

M Left foot remains in place, weight is taken onto it, turning to right.

L Right foot remains in place, weight is taken onto it, turning to right.

3

count: three

M **Left foot** to side of right foot with part weight on foot.

L **Right foot** to side of left foot with part weight on foot.

Both turn to face partner.

4

count: four

M **Left foot** remains in place and weight is taken fully onto it.

L **Right foot** remains in place and weight is taken fully onto it.

7

count: three

M **Right foot** to side of left foot with part weight on foot.

L **Left foot** to side of right foot with part weight on foot.

Both turn to face partner.

8

count: four

M **Right foot** remains in place and weight taken fully onto it.

L **Left foot** remains in place and weight taken fully onto it.

Man and Lady Twirls

The figure starts after the Cucaracha Steps, Forwards and Backwards Basics or Outside Breaks (see pages 116–19, 120–23 and 128–31). There is a fair amount of turning in this twirling dance (albeit not too difficult) and it helps to try to visualise the sequence before practising it (see box opposite).

count: **Man's Steps**

one 1 **Left foot** takes a small step forwards and across the body, turning slightly right. Release hold of the lady from your right hand, raise your left hand up over her head to form an arch and start turning her to the left by making an anticlockwise rotation of the left hand. Do not grip the lady's hand too firmly.

two 2 **Right foot** closes near to left foot turning a little to the left, still turning the lady to her left.

three-four 3 **Left foot** marks time drawing your left and the lady's right hand a little towards you, preparing for your turn. The step takes twice as long as the previous two steps.

one 4 **Right foot** marks time on the ball of the foot, starting to turn to the left under the arch. To turn sufficiently, swivel on the right foot.

two 5 **Left foot** marks time, continue turning strongly to the left, swivelling on the ball of your foot.

three-four 6 **Right foot** marks time, completing the turn to the left, lower your left hand and regain normal position.

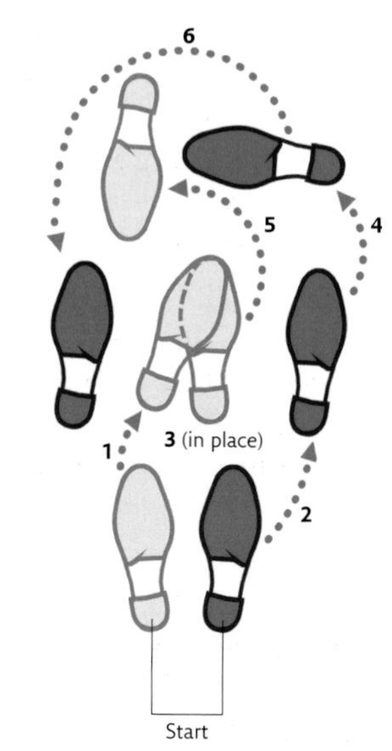

must know

Imagine the sequence
The man releases the lady from his right hand and guides her into a strong turn to the left, under his left and her right hand, for the first four beats. On the second four beats, she continues to turn but not so strongly. At the end of the second four beats, partners face each other again. The man makes a little turn to the right and then to the left, on the first four beats, then makes a strong turn to the left under the raised hands, on the second four beats.

Lady's Steps

count:	
one	1 **Right foot** takes a small step to the side on the ball of your foot, turning strongly to the left. The man will raise his left and your right hand to create an arch, under which first you and then he will turn. Allow your right hand to turn in the man's left hand. To turn sufficiently swivel on the balls of the feet.
two	2 **Left foot** closes to right foot, still turning strongly to the left.
three-four	3 **Right foot** marks time, continuing the strong turn to the left.
one	4 **Left foot** marks time, continuing to turn slightly to the left, allowing the man to start his turn to the left under the arch.
two	5 **Right foot** marks time, the man is turning under the arch. You should now be facing your partner's back.
three-four	6 **Left foot** marks time, lower your right hand and regain normal hold.

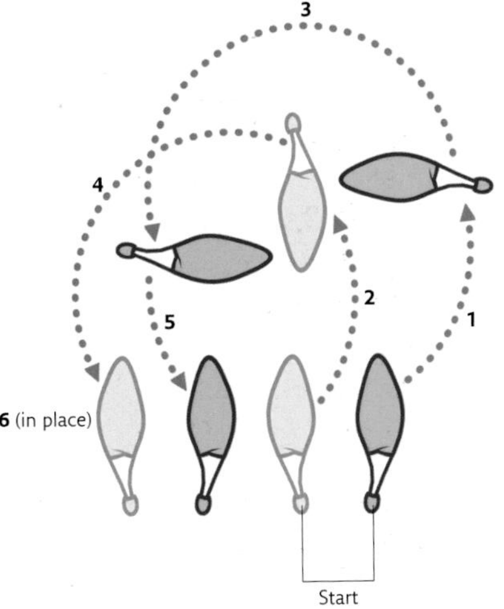

Man and Lady Twirls

1

count: one

M Left foot forwards and across, turn slightly to right, raise hand and start to turn the lady left.

L Right foot to side, turn strongly to the left under arch.

2

count: two

M Right foot closes near to left foot turning a little to the left, still turning the lady to her left.

L Left foot closes to right foot, still turning strongly to the left.

4

count: one

M Right foot marks time on ball of foot, starting strong turn to the left under the arch formed.

L Left foot marks time, still turning slightly to the left.

5

count: two

M Left foot marks time, still turning strongly to the left and swivelling on ball of foot.

L Right foot marks time, partner is still turning under the arch.

3

count: three-four

M Left foot marks time, drawing your left and the lady's right hand a little towards you.

L Right foot marks time, still turning strongly to the left.

6

count: three-four

M Right foot marks time, completing the turn to the left, lower left hand, regain normal position.

L Left foot marks time, lower right hand and regain normal hold.

want to know more?

- Join a Salsa club, see local newspapers, Yellow Pages and the Internet for addresses.
- Check with your local authority for Latin dance evening classes.
- See listings of dance studios on pages 184–9.

weblinks

- Look up Salsa on en.wikipedia.org/wiki/Salsa for information on different styles of Salsa.
- For listings and articles visit www.uksalsa.com
- For instructional videos visit www.activevideos.com/salsa.htm
- For free downloads of some steps visit www.salsa-merengue.co.uk
- Find out more about Salsa music visit www.salsaand merengue.com

6 Merengue

This is a delightfully simple dance form that relies on very small steps and swinging the hips over each foot as weight is transferred. It is danced at a brisk pace to music that is less complicated than that of most Caribbean countries, and in the simpler figures each step takes one beat of music. However, the man still needs to lead the lady to the figures and in some ways the fact that there is little movement over the floor makes this even more essential.

A vibrant dance

In many ways the Merengue, sometimes called Meringue, has the simplest basic rhythm and form of all Latin dances. It is a vibrant, brisk and exciting dance.

Both the Dominican Republic and Haiti claim the dance originated with them. However, the distinction is perhaps less significant than it might otherwise seem. They form the two halves of the Caribbean island originally called Hispaniola, which was the first part of the New World discovered by Christopher Columbus in December 1492. The dance has also been performed for many years in Venezuela on the northern coast of the mainland of the South American continent, and is now gaining in popularity worldwide.

did you know?

What's in a name

The origin of the Spanish name 'merengue' is not clear. It translates in English to 'meringue' - a light and frothy confection of whipped egg white and sugar. Some believe that the name was chosen because of the character of the dance, which is also light and frothy.

Cultural background

The ethnic background differs. The background of the Dominican Republic is Spanish or mixed Spanish and African descent with Spanish as the national language. In Haiti, the population is largely of African descent with a sizeable French influence as can be seen by the fact that the official language is French. In Venezuela, three-quarters of the population are Mestizos (of Spanish and native American origins) and the heritage other than that of Native Americans is Spanish, as is the official language. The dance first made an impact in Western culture in the USA in the early 1950s, and by the 1970s was well established in American ballrooms. Within the last ten years or so it has become popular in the UK.

Originally the dance was performed with a 'limping' action for which fanciful explanations abound. One suggests that it was a dance popular with slaves who, having been chained together by one ankle, tended to drag the opposite leg. Another myth is that a popular army general had been wounded in one leg and dancers started to limp in sympathy with him. There is no evidence to confirm either of these stories and, generally, they are regarded as spurious. Nevertheless, at one time the dance was performed with a limping action.

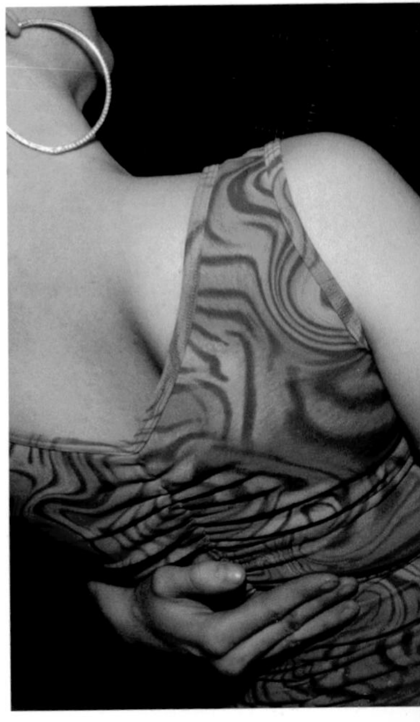

For the basic Merengue figures dancers adopt a close body contact hold.

Music and rhythmic patterns

For a Latin American dance the musical base is deceptively simple and, while it may be written in 4/4, 2/4, 2/2 or even 6/8 time signatures, we use 4/4 time with one step taken on each beat of the bar of music. There are subtle, syncopated, rhythmic patterns or rolls played by accompanying instruments that help to create the feeling of drive that is typical of the music. All figures will be counted 'One, two, three, four' in groups of four steps covering one bar of 4/4 music.

The hold and hip action

The modern dance is performed slower than in earlier days with no limping action. However, the hip action so typical of the Latin dances of South America is evident and essential. The hold for the simpler figures is a close body contact hold, with the man's right arm well around the lady. His left hand is higher than in other close contact dances and can be level with the top of his head. His left elbow is brought a little further forwards than in other dances. When you are comfortable with the simpler figures, various open holds can be used, such as when the man holds the lady's hands in his hands. This can be the lady's right hand in the man's left and the lady's left hand in the man's right, or vice versa.

Forwards and Backwards Basics

You can dance this figure facing any direction in the room. The first four steps can be repeated once before going into step 5, and then steps 5–8 can follow. The figure takes two bars of 4/4 music. Remember to listen to the rhythm.

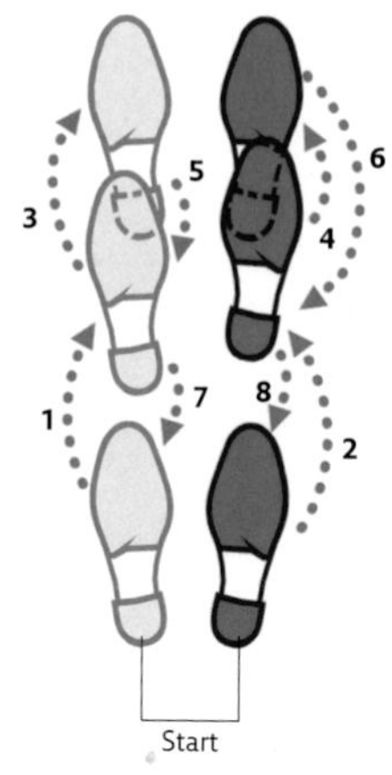

count:		**Man's Steps**
one	1	**Left foot** takes a step forwards.
two	2	**Right foot** takes a step forwards.
three	3	**Left foot** takes a step forwards.
four	4	**Right foot** closes to side of left foot.
one	5	**Left foot** takes a step backwards.
two	6	**Right foot** takes a step backwards.
three	7	**Left foot** takes a step backwards.
four	8	**Right foot** closes to side of left foot.

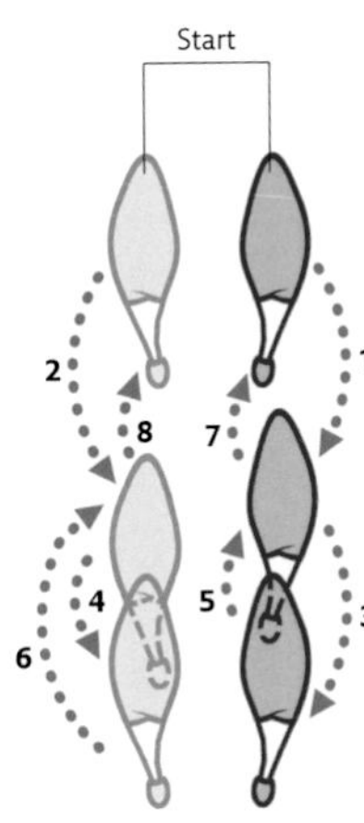

Lady's Steps

count:		
one	1	**Right foot** takes a step backwards.
two	2	**Left foot** takes a step backwards.
three	3	**Right foot** takes a step backwards.
four	4	**Left foot** closes to side of right foot.
one	5	**Right foot** takes a step forwards.
two	6	**Left foot** takes a step forwards.
three	7	**Right foot** takes a step forwards.
four	8	**Left foot** closes to side of right foot.

must know

Swinging hips

As every step is completed, the hips swing sideways over the foot that has just moved into position. For example, if you start with the weight over the right foot as the left foot takes a step (in any direction) when the foot reaches the position, the weight settles onto it and the hips move leftwards.

Remember:

- **The waist should be kept fluid and the shoulders steady, giving the feeling that the dance is taking part mainly in the area of the waist and hips.**
- **This swinging of the hips takes place on every step and will not be described in the figures that follow, but nevertheless is vital for a good dance interpretation.**
- **All the steps in this dance are small and, indeed, should not move out of the area covered by the trunk of the body.**

Forwards and Backwards Basics

1

count: one

M Left foot takes a step forwards.

L Right foot takes a step backwards.

2

count: two

M Right foot takes a step forwards.

L Left foot takes a step backwards.

5

count: one

M Left foot takes a step backwards.

L Right foot takes a step forwards.

6

count: two

M Right foot takes a step backwards.

L Left foot takes a step forwards.

3

count: three

M **Left foot** takes a step forwards.

L **Right foot** takes a step backwards.

4

count: four

M **Right foot** closes to side of left foot.

L **Left foot** closes to side of right foot.

7

count: three

M **Left foot** takes a step backwards.

L **Right foot** takes a step forwards.

8

count: four

M **Right foot** closes to side of left foot.

L **Left foot** closes to side of right foot.

Progressive Chassés

This figure can follow the Forwards and Backwards Basics (see pages 140–3) and, while it can be danced facing any direction, for preference the man should face the nearest wall with the lady facing him with her back towards the nearest wall.

Do not be misled by the term 'Progressive'. There is a little progression to the side but it is very small and must not overshadow the lateral swing of the hips from left to right and vice versa. The figure takes two bars of 4/4 music.

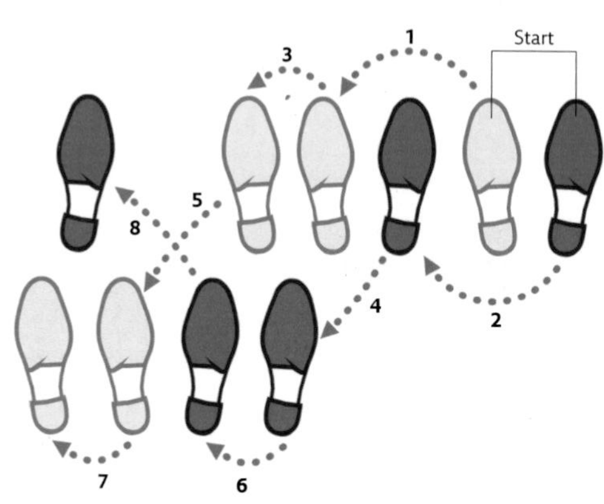

count:		**Man's Steps**
one	1	**Left foot** takes a step to the side.
two	2	**Right foot** closes towards left foot.
three	3	**Left foot** takes a step to the side.
four	4	**Right foot** takes a step backwards.
one	5	**Left foot** takes a step to the side.
two	6	**Right foot** closes towards left foot.
three	7	**Left foot** takes a step to the side.
four	8	**Right foot** takes a step forwards.

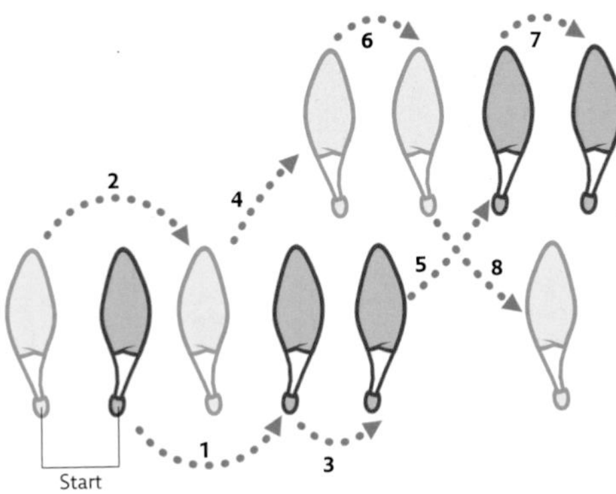

count: **Lady's Steps**

count		
one	1	**Right foot** takes a step to the side.
two	2	**Left foot** closes towards right foot.
three	3	**Right foot** takes a step to the side.
four	4	**Left foot** takes a step forwards.
one	5	**Right foot** takes a step to the side.
two	6	**Left foot** closes towards right foot.
three	7	**Right foot** takes a step to the side.
four	8	**Left foot** takes a step backwards.

must know

Variation

Once you have mastered the steps of this figure without turn, try turning them gently clockwise, that is, to your right. Remember to take small steps with a strong lateral hip swing.

Progressive Chassés

1

count: one

M Left foot takes a step to the side.

L Right foot takes a step to the side.

2

count: two

M Right foot closes towards left foot.

L Left foot closes towards right foot.

5

count: one

M Left foot takes a step to the side.

L Right foot takes a step to the side.

6

count: two

M Right foot closes towards left foot.

L Left foot closes towards right foot.

3

count: three

M **Left foot** takes a step to the side.

L **Right foot** takes a step to the side.

4

count: four

M **Right foot** takes a step backwards.

L **Left foot** takes a step forwards.

7

count: three

M **Left foot** takes a step to the side.

L **Right foot** takes a step to the side.

8

count: four

M **Right foot** takes a step forwards.

L **Left foot** takes a step backwards.

Continued Zig Zag

This figure can precede or follow any Merengue figure described in this book. It is important to keep the steps 'outside partner' short. After step 5 has been taken you can repeat steps 2–5 (inclusive), then continue with steps 6–8.

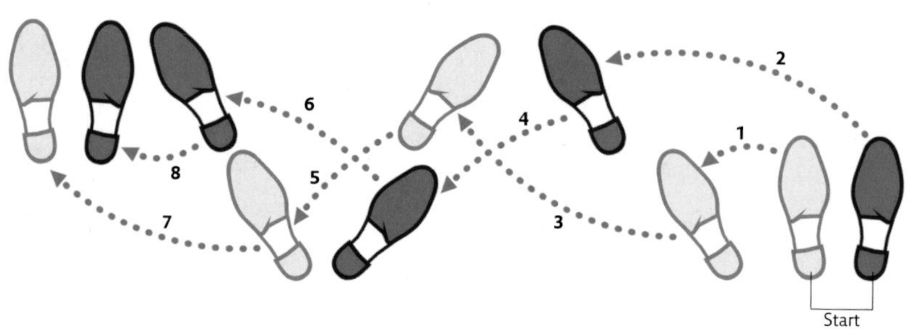

Man's Steps

count:		
one	1	**Left foot** takes a step to the side, turning to the left.
two	2	**Right foot** takes a step forwards in front and across the left foot, to your left of your partner (a position dancers call 'outside partner').
three	3	**Left foot** takes a step to the side, turning to the right with partner in normal position in front of you.
four	4	**Right foot** takes a step backwards behind and across the left foot, guiding partner to take a step forwards on your left side (a position dancers call 'partner outside').
one	5	**Left foot** takes a step to the side, turning to the left with partner in normal position in front of you.
two	6	**Right foot** takes a step forwards in front and across the left foot, to your left of your partner ('outside partner').
three	7	**Left foot** takes a step to the side, turning to the right with partner in normal position in front of you.
four	8	**Right foot** closes to left foot.

must know

Like the Continued Zig Zag, each of the figures described in the Merengue section can precede or follow each other.

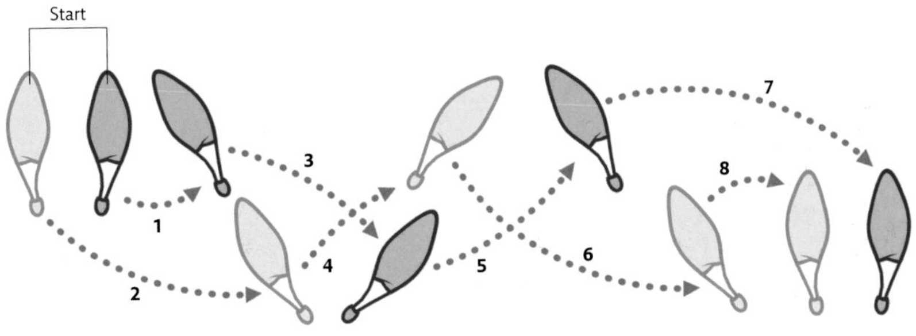

count:

Lady's Steps

one **1** Right foot takes a step to the side, turning slightly to the left.

two **2** Left foot takes a step backwards behind and across the right foot with partner on your right side ('partner outside').

three **3** Right foot takes a step to the side, turning to the right with partner in normal position in front of you.

four **4** Left foot takes a step forwards in front and across right foot to your right side of your partner's feet ('outside partner').

one **5** Right foot takes a step to the side, turning to the left with partner in normal position in front of you.

two **6** Left foot takes a step backwards behind and across the right foot with partner on your right side ('partner outside').

three **7** Right foot takes a step to the side, turning to the right with partner in normal position in front of you

four **8** Left foot closes to right foot.

Continued Zig Zag

1
count: one

M Left foot takes a step to the side, turning to the left.

L Right foot takes a step to the side, turning slightly to the left.

2
count: two

M Right foot takes a step forwards in front and across the left foot, to your left of your partner ('outside partner').

L Left foot takes a step backwards and across the right foot with partner on your right side ('partner outside').

5
count: one

M Left foot takes a step to the side, turning to the left to face partner.

L Right foot takes a step to the side, turning to the left to face partner.

6
count: two

M Right foot takes a step forwards in front and across left foot, to your left of your partner ('outside partner').

L Left foot takes a step backwards and across the right foot with partner on your right side ('partner outside').

3

count: three

M **Left foot** takes a step to the side, turning to the right to face partner.

L **Right foot** takes a step to the side, turning to the right to face partner.

4

count: four

M **Right foot** takes a step backwards and across the left foot, guiding partner to take a step forwards on your left side ('partner outside').

L **Left foot** takes a step forwards and across the right foot to your right side of your partner's feet ('outside partner').

7

count: three

M **Left foot** takes a step to the side, turning to the right to face partner.

L **Right foot** takes a step to the side, turning to the right to face partner.

8

count: four

M **Right foot** closes to left foot.

L **Left foot** closes to right foot.

The Wheel

In this figure the couple rotates in a circle around a central point much as the spokes of a wheel turn. The figure can be extended by repeating steps 9 and 10 as many times as you wish before moving on to steps 11–16.

count: **Man's Steps**

one **1** **Left foot** takes a step to the side.

two **2** **Right foot** closes to left foot lowering left hand to roughly waist level.

three **3** **Left foot** takes a step backwards, pushing partner away from you with left hand still held at waist level and releasing hold of her back with right hand. Keep left hand relaxed and do not grip partner's hand when guiding her.

four **4** **Right foot** closes to left foot, taking hold of partner's left hand in your right hand at waist level.

one **5** **Left foot** takes a step to the side, turning a little to the left. Your right arm straightens a little so as to guide partner to turn to her left.

two **6** **Right foot** closes to left foot, still turning a little to the left.

three **7** **Left foot** takes a step to the side, still turning a little to the left.

four **8** **Right foot** closes to left foot, still turning to the left, by now your right shoulder should be pointing to and in line with partner's right shoulder. You will have turned about 90 degrees to the left from starting position. Over the next six steps (steps 9–14) you will turn to the right to bring you facing partner again.

one **9** **Left foot** takes a step forwards, beginning to turn right and curving to the right.

two **10** **Right foot** takes a step forwards, turning to the right and curving to the right.

three **11** **Left foot** takes a step forwards, turning to the right and curving to the right.

four **12** **Right foot** takes a step forwards, turning to the right, pushing left hand forwards and pulling right hand backwards so as to start turning your partner more strongly to the right.

one **13** **Left foot** takes a step to the side, completing turn to the right and bringing partner to face you.

two **14** **Right foot** takes a step forwards, moving towards partner.

three **15** **Left foot** takes a step to the side, regaining normal hold.

four **16** **Right foot** closes to left foot.

must know

More complex
The Wheel may seem to be a more difficult figure. However, do not be put off – it is a typical rotational figure. Follow the instructions a few steps at a time and then join these smaller units together and you will find it will all work out.

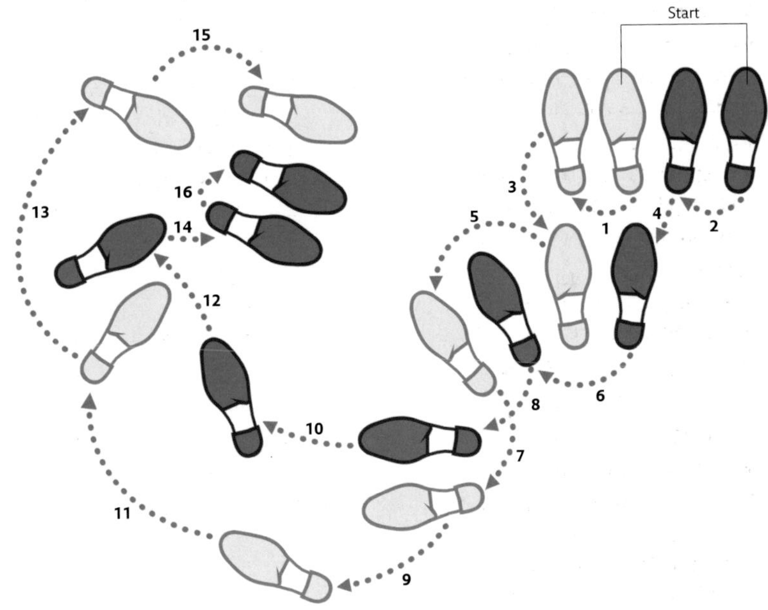

The Wheel (continued)

count: **Lady's Steps**

one 1 **Right foot** takes a step to the side.

two 2 **Left foot** closes to right foot, partner will lower his left and your right hand to roughly waist level.

three 3 **Right foot** takes a step backwards, partner will release hold of your body with his right hand.

four 4 **Left foot** closes to right foot, partner will take hold of your left hand in his right at waist level.

one 5 **Right foot** takes a step to the side, turning a little to the left. Your right arm starts to straighten so as to allow you to turn to your left.

two 6 **Left foot** closes to right foot, still turning to the left.

three 7 **Right foot** takes a step to the side, still turning to the left.

four 8 **Left foot** closes to right foot, still turning to the left, by now your right shoulder should be pointing to and in line with the man's right shoulder.

one 9 **Right foot** takes a step forwards, beginning to turn right and curving to the right.

two 10 **Left foot** takes a step forwards, turning to the right and curving to the right.

three 11 **Right foot** takes a step forwards, turning to the right and curving to the right.

four 12 **Left foot** takes a step forwards, turning more strongly to the right. Partner will be pushing your right hand backwards and pulling left hand forwards so as to start turning you to face him.

one 13 **Right foot** takes a step to the side, completing the turn to the right to bring you facing partner.

two 14 **Left foot** takes a step forwards, moving towards partner.

three 15 **Right foot** takes a step to the side, regaining normal hold.

four 16 **Left foot** closes to right foot.

must know

When there is strong turn the hip action should still be applied but inevitably it will be rather less than on non-turning figures, however it should not be lost entirely.

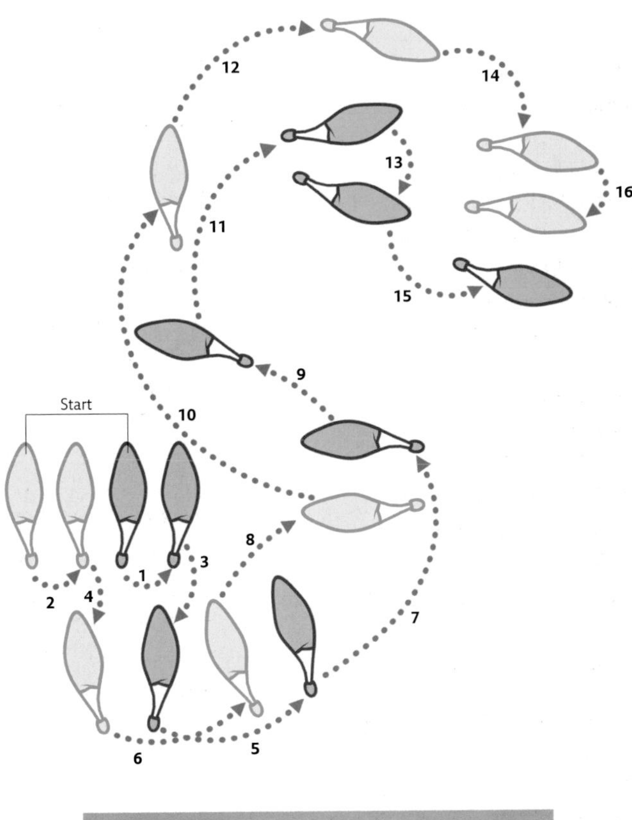

The Wheel

1

count: one

M **Left foot** takes a step to the side.

L **Right foot** takes a step to the side.

2

count: two

M **Right foot** closes to left foot, lowering left hand roughly to waist level.

L **Left foot** closes to right foot, partner will lower his left and your right hand roughly to waist level.

5

count: one

M **Left foot** to the side, turning left a little and guiding lady to turn to her left.

L **Right foot** to the side. Your right arm starts to straighten allowing you to turn to the left.

6

count: two

M **Right foot** closes to left foot, still turning a little to the left.

L **Left foot** closes to right foot, still turning to the left.

3

count: three

M **Left foot** takes a step backwards, pushing partner away from you with left hand and releasing hold of her back with right hand.

L **Right foot** takes a step backwards, partner will release hold of your body with his right hand.

4

count: four

M **Right foot** closes to left foot, taking hold of partner's left hand in your right hand at waist level.

L **Left foot** closes to right foot, partner will take hold of your left hand in his right at waist level.

7

count: three

M **Left foot** takes a step to the side, still turning a little to the left.

L **Right foot** takes a step to the side, still turning to the left.

8

count: four

M **Right foot** closes to left foot, still turning to the left, now with your right shoulder in line with partner's.

L **Left foot** closes towards right foot, still turning to the left, now with your right shoulder in line with partner's.

The Wheel (continued)

9

count: one

M Left foot takes a step forwards, beginning to turn right and curving to the right.

L Right foot takes a step forwards, beginning to turn right and curving to the right.

10

count: two

M Right foot takes a step forwards, turning to the right and curving to the right.

L Left foot takes a step forwards, turning to the right and curving to the right.

13

count: one

M Left foot takes a step to the side, completing turn to the right and bringing partner to face you.

L Right foot takes a step to the side, completing the turn to the right to bring you facing partner.

14

count: two

M Right foot takes a step forwards, moving towards partner.

L Left foot takes a step forwards, moving towards partner.

11
count: three

M **Left foot** takes a step forwards, turning to the right and curving to the right.

L **Right foot** takes a step forwards, turning to the right and curving to the right.

12
count: four

M **Right foot** takes a step forwards, pushing left hand forwards, pulling right hand backwards, and guiding partner to turn to the right.

L **Left foot** takes a step forwards, turning more strongly to the right.

15
count: three

M **Left foot** takes a step to the side, regaining normal hold.

L **Right foot** takes a step to the side, regaining normal hold.

16
count: four

M **Right foot** closes to left foot.

L **Left foot** closes to right foot.

Separation and Reunion

In this figure the man and lady move backwards away from each other and then draw together again. It is important to remember that the steps are all small.

The figure can be danced from the Close Hold or from the Open Hold (see pages 14–15), allowing the lady to dance a little distance away from partner.

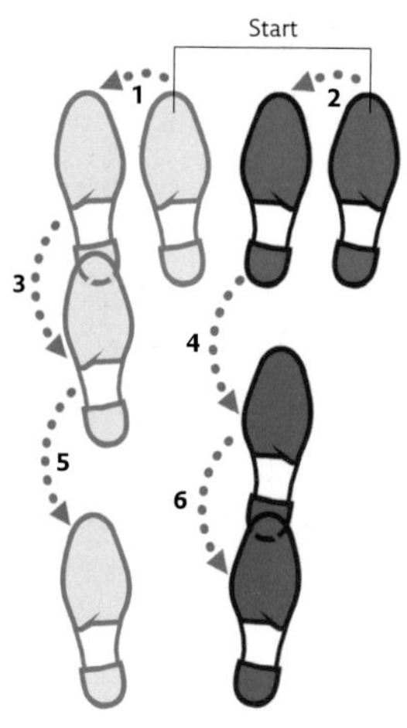

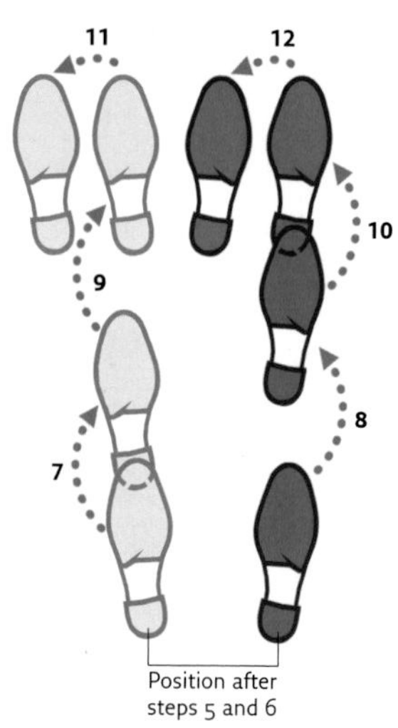

count:

Man's Steps

one 1 **Left foot** takes a step to the side.

two 2 **Right foot** closes towards left foot, lowering left hand to waist level.

three 3 **Left foot** takes a step backwards, pushing partner away from you, keeping left hand at waist level, but releasing hold with right hand. Keep left hand relaxed.

four 4 **Right foot** takes a step backwards.

one 5 **Left foot** takes a step backwards.

two 6 **Right foot** closes to left foot, checking partner's backwards movement by lightly pulling on her right hand with your left hand.

three 7 **Left foot** takes a step forwards, pulling partner towards you with your left hand that is still holding her right hand at waist level.

four 8 **Right foot** takes a step forwards, gently pulling partner towards you.

one 9 **Left foot** takes a step forwards, gently pulling partner towards you.

two 10 **Right foot** closes to left foot regaining normal hold.

three 11 **Left foot** takes a step to the side.

four 12 **Right foot** closes to left foot.

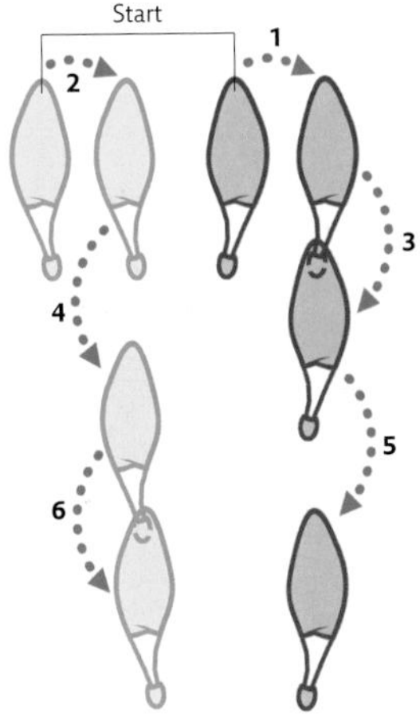

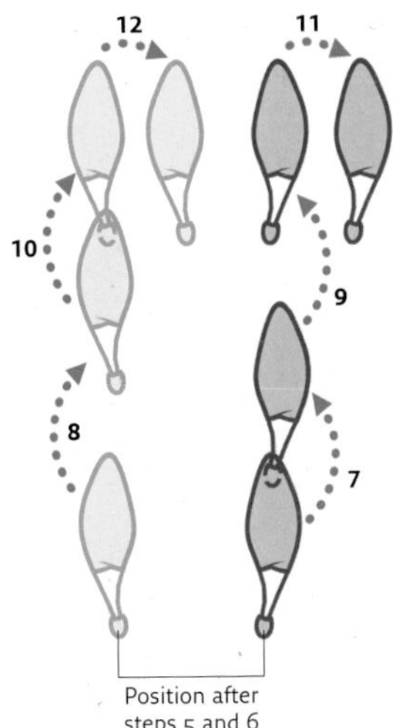

Lady's Steps

count:		
one	1	**Right foot** takes a step to the side.
two	2	**Left foot** closes towards right foot, partner will lower his left hand and your right hand on this step.
three	3	**Right foot** takes a step backwards, releasing hold of partner with your left hand responding to him lowering his left hand and then pushing on your right hand.
four	4	**Left foot** takes a step backwards.
one	5	**Right foot** takes a step backwards.
two	6	**Left foot** closes to right foot, partner will retain hold of your right hand.
three	7	**Right foot** takes a step forwards towards partner.
four	8	**Left foot** takes a step forwards towards partner.
one	9	**Right foot** takes a step forwards towards partner.
two	10	**Left foot** closes to right foot regaining normal hold.
three	11	**Right foot** takes a step to the side.
four	12	**Left foot** closes to right foot.

Separation and Reunion

1

count: one

M Left foot takes a step to the side.

L Right foot takes a step to the side.

2

count: two

M Right foot closes towards left foot, lowering left hand to waist level.

L Left foot closes towards right foot, partner will lower his left hand and your right hand on this step.

4

count: four

M Right foot takes a step backwards.

L Left foot takes a step backwards.

5

count: one

M Left foot takes a step backwards.

L Right foot takes a step backwards.

3

count: three

M **Left foot** takes a step backwards, pushing partner away from you, keeping left hand at waist level but releasing hold with right hand.

L **Right foot** takes a step backwards, releasing hold of partner with your left hand responding to him lowering his left hand and pushing on your right hand.

6

count: two

M **Right foot** closes to left foot, checking partner's backwards movement by lightly pulling on her right hand with your left hand.

L **Left foot** closes to right foot.

(continued overleaf)

must know

Adding movement

This enhancement can follow the Separation and Reunion and is best taken in the Open Hold. When you are confident with the figure, the man can try turning to the left and the lady to the right on steps 3–5, with the man releasing hold of the lady's right hand from his left hand as they move away from one another. The steps move in a sideways direction. On steps 7–9 the man will turn to the right and the lady to the left, the man will regain hold of the lady's right hand in his left on the steps moving forwards towards partner. Normal hold will be regained on step 10.

Separation and Reunion (continued)

7

count: three

M Left foot takes a step forwards, pulling partner towards you with your left hand that is still holding her right hand at waist level.

L Right foot takes a step forwards towards partner.

8

count: four

M Right foot takes a step forwards, gently pulling partner towards you.

L Left foot takes a step forwards towards partner.

10

count: two

M Right foot closes to left foot regaining normal hold.

L Left foot closes to right foot regaining normal hold.

11

count: three

M Left foot takes a step to the side.

L Right foot takes a step to the side.

9

count: one

M Left foot takes a step forwards, gently pulling partner towards you.

L Right foot takes a step forwards towards partner.

12

count: four

M Right foot closes to left foot.

L Left foot closes to right foot.

want to know more?

- Join a dance school, see local newspapers, Yellow Pages and listing of dance studios on pages 184–9.
- Salsa clubs often feature Merengue. Many include guidance from instructors prior to the evening's dancing.

weblinks

- For tutorials visit www.salsa-merengue.co.uk
- To find out more about Merengue music visit www.salasaand merengue.com
- For a selection of instructional videos visit www.activevideos.com
- For help in finding a dance school visit www.danceweb.co.uk and see the websites of dance teachers' organisations as listed on pages 183–4.

7 Disco/Freestyle

This is the dance of the club culture and can be whatever takes the dancer's fancy. It helps if you can express what you feel the music is urging you to do and not be too concerned with specific 'steps' or figures. Nevertheless, the simple actions that we describe will help to give you a feel for what forms the foundation of the solo dance that is disco. An essential component of every dance is the music, and this is particularly true of Disco dancing. Listen to the beat – you can hardly fail to do so.

Club culture

To the uninitiated, Disco dancing can often look like completely wild and undisciplined movements of the limbs, but to aficionados this dance form is capable of analysis.

Among the current popular dances, Disco, also called Freestyle, is different from most in that it is danced solo. Also, it is not danced to a set sequence, as is the case in line dancing, for example. With the exception of specialist clubs that feature Salsa, Argentine Tango, and so on, Disco is the dance of the club culture. However, the music is all-pervasive and everyone can learn and enjoy the dance in a way that will give the fullest enjoyment of the expression of the music.

Movement

As might be expected, it is necessary to approach the dance in a rather different way from that employed for the traditional forms of ballroom dancing. Each part of the body is involved. Movements can be made in four fundamental ways: turning or rotating, tilting, lifting and bending. These actions can apply to almost any part of the body – head, arms, legs and body torso. This is best illustrated with a few examples.

Turning your head to look left or right are examples of 'turning'. Keeping the eyeline straight in front and then tilting the head to look up and dropping the chin down onto the chest are 'tilting'. Raising your shoulders as in shrugging is 'lifting'. Bending the arm at the elbow is 'bending'. All these actions fit to the strong beat of the music and usually take place concurrently on the same beat of music. The following basic units will get you started and you are in the happy position of not needing a partner and only needing the minimum of space.

Disco dancing took off in the 1970s. One of the most fashionable clubs was Studio 54 in New York.

The 'steps'

Unlike other dances there are no universally agreed 'movements' in Disco. In this section there are a few basic routines to get you started, and they have been given names purely as an aid to memory. Again, unlike other dances, the steps are the same for the man and the lady. In all descriptions each 'step' takes one beat of music. Try the basics that follow to slow music first, until you are sure that you can dance them, and then gradually increase the music speed. Because this is an entirely non-progressive dance you can face in any direction for the various figures.

Head Turns

Start with the feet slightly apart, with the weight over your right foot, looking forwards with both hands held loosely at the sides of the body. The eight steps that follow take eight beats of music in 4/4 time and use legs and head only.

1

count: one

Left foot takes a small step to the side without weight, with toe pointed to the floor and heel slightly raised. Keep the weight on right foot and turn head left, with arms at your side.

2

count: two

Left foot closes back to the starting position near to right foot. Keep the weight on right foot and turn head forwards, with arms still at your side.

5

count: one

Right foot takes a small step to the side without weight, with toe pointed. Keep the weight on left foot and turn your head to the right, with arms at your side.

6

count: two

Right foot closes back to the starting position near to left foot. Keep the weight on left foot and turn your head forwards, with arms still at your side.

3

count: three

Repeat step 1.

4

count: four

Repeat step 2 but take the weight onto the left foot.

7

count: three

Repeat step 5.

8

count: four

Repeat step 6 but take the weight onto the right foot.

Head Turns and Hand Movement

You will see that this is merely the Head Turns figure (see pages 170–1) with the addition of simple hand actions that will help your co-ordination. Start with the weight on your right foot. Each movement or step takes one beat of music.

1

count: one

Left foot takes a small step to the side. Keep the weight on the right foot with toe pointed to the floor and turn head to the left, raising left hand upwards.

2

count: two

Left foot closes back to the starting position. Keep the weight on the right foot and turn your head to look forwards again, with arms at the side of your body.

5

count: one

Right foot takes a small step to the side, with toe pointed towards the floor. Keep the weight on left foot and turn your head to the right, raising your right hand upwards.

6

count: two

Right foot closes back to the starting position. Keep the weight on the left foot and turn your head to look forwards again, with arms at the side of your body.

3

count: three

Repeat step 1.

4

count: four

Repeat step 2 but take the weight onto the left foot.

7

count: three

Repeat step 5.

8

count: four

Repeat step 6 but take the weight onto the right foot.

Springy Knees

The bending of the knee should take place on the heaviest beats in the bar of music and you should experiment until you feel what you are doing fits the music best. As an alternative, you can pause on the first beat of music, then bend your knees on the second beat. Start with the weight on both your feet.

1

count: one

Bend both knees.

2

count: two

Straighten knees.

3

count: three

Bend both knees.

4

count: four

Straighten knees.

Hip Rolls

The Hip Roll is described as rotating right first but you can rotate left first. Raw beginners can take one beat of music for each of the counts but, as soon as possible, try to speed this up, until you can complete one full rotation in two beats of music. Start with the weight on both your feet. Then repeat the action.

1

count: one

Push your hips forwards with your knees bent and weight over both feet.

2

count: two

Rotate the hips to the right side with a circular movement.

3

count: three

Pull the hips backwards.

4

count: four

Rotate the hips to the left side, with a circular movement.

Head, Hands, Feet and Knees

This group of steps brings together several of the basic actions detailed in the other Disco movements. Start with the weight on the right foot with knees slightly bent. Each movement or step takes one beat of music.

1

count: one

Left foot takes a small step forwards and to the side, keeping weight on right foot. Push left hip upwards and forwards, turn head left and raise left hand upwards.

2

count: two

Left foot closes to right foot, still keeping weight on right foot and bringing hips back to normal position. Turn your head forwards and lower your hand and arm to your side.

5

count: one

Right foot takes a small step forwards and to the side, keeping weight on left foot. Push right hip upwards and forwards, turn head right and raise right hand upwards.

6

count: two

Right foot closes to left foot, still keeping weight on left foot and bringing the hips back to normal position. Turn your head forwards and lower your hand and arm to your side.

3

count: three

Repeat step 1.

4

count: four

Left foot closes to right foot taking the weight back onto it and bringing the hips back to normal position. Turn your head forwards and lower your hand and arm to your side.

7

count: three

Repeat step 5.

8

count: four

Right foot closes to left foot, taking weight back onto it, and bringing the hips back to the normal position. Turn your head forwards and lower your hand and arm to your side.

Shoulder Shimmy or Boob Trembler

When you are really comfortable with the figure, the more lissom of you can add the Hip Rolls (see pages 175) or hoola hoop type movements.

Start with the weight equally placed over both feet and knees slightly bent. Hold the hands forwards so that the forearms are roughly parallel to the floor but also relaxed.

1

count: one

Right shoulder forwards and left shoulder backwards. Takes one beat of music.

2

count: two

Left shoulder forwards and right shoulder backwards. Takes one beat of music.

Faster Shoulder Shimmy or Boob Trembler

Left shoulder forwards then right shoulder forwards on the count of 'one' and repeat for each count. This is double the speed of the Shoulder Shimmy on the opposite page, but even this is not fast enough.

Try to double the speed again until you can fit the 'left, right, left, right' combination to each beat of music.

did you know?

What's in a name
The name Disco is short for the French word discothèque. The first was opened in Paris in the late-1940s under the name Whiskey à Go-Go. It was the death knell of the British dance halls (often referred to as *Palais de Danse*) with their very large dance floors.

1

count: one

Left shoulder forwards.

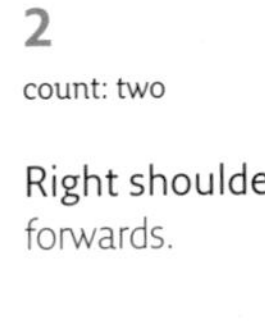

2

count: two

Right shoulder forwards.

The Twist

Solo dancing became popular in the 1960s when Chubby Checker released the pop records, 'Let's Twist' and 'Let's Twist Again'. It is a while ago now, but the basic movement is still seen on the dancing scene and it is well within the reach of inexperienced dancers.

Start with the feet slightly apart, with the weight on both feet and with your knees slightly bent. Hold your hands at about waist level, a little in front of the body. It might help to imagine that you are holding something, say a small book, between them or even holding one hand in the other.

Repeat steps 1 and 2 as many times as you fancy.

must know

Twist again

Add a little spice to the action by bending the knees more and more until you are nearly kneeling on the floor (see 4 below).

1

count: one

Take weight forwards onto balls of feet without raising the heels from floor. Turn on balls of feet so that heels shift to left and toes point to right, move your hands leftwards.

3

count: three

Repeat step 1 then step 2. Repeat these steps as often as you wish.

4

variation

Add spice to the action – continue twisting until your knees are fully bent and you are close to the floor. Your arms should help you to balance.

2

count: two

With weight on the balls of the feet, turn so that the heels move to the right and the toes point to left, at the same time move your hands rightwards.

5

twist again

Gradually twist yourself up to the starting position, ready to 'twist again'.

want to know more?

- Subscribe to a social dance magazine such as *Dance Expression*, or *Dance Today!*
- For dance studios see pages 184–9.
- Films to inspire you – *Dirty Dancing*, *Footloose* and *Saturday Night Fever*.

weblinks

- To find out more about Disco music visit www.discomusic.com or www.disco-disco.com
- For a selection of instructional videos visit www.activevideos.com
- For help in finding a dance school visit www.danceweb.co.uk
- To learn more about the Twist visit www.centralhome.com/ballroomcountry/twist.htm

Glossary

Backing line of dance: When the dancer is backing the imaginary line of dance (see Line of dance) then he or she is 'backing line of dance'.

Dance patterns: The various steps and figures used in dancing make patterns on the floor that are called 'dance patterns'.

Facing diagonally to wall: This is an indication of where the dancer is in relation to the movement of the dance. Face the line of dance (see below), then turn 45 degrees to the right to be 'facing diagonally to wall'.

Facing line of dance: Face the imaginary line defined as the line of dance (see below).

Fall-away position: For Latin dances, stand in the promenade position, then the man's left foot takes a step backwards and the lady's right foot takes a step backwards.

Fast syncopation: Syncopation is variance of the basic rhythm either by changing the emphasis or interloping additional beats or omitting beats. 'Fast syncopation' in dance happens when a string of rapidly interpolated steps are inserted into the basic rhythmic pattern.

Figure: A series of steps linked together as one unit.

Foot marks time in place: The foot remains in place but the weight of your body is transferred onto it.

Foot remains in place: The foot remains in the position previously achieved and the weight of your body is retained on it.

4/4 time: A musical term, sometimes called common time, to indicate that there are four crotchets, or beats, in each bar of music.

Hip action: Movement of the hips from the waist down. Mostly laterally from left to right but can be forwards and backwards.

Line of dance: This an imaginary line parallel with the wall along which the dance moves. The dance progresses in an anti-clockwise direction around the room, and in a rectangular room it turns 90 degrees at each corner.

Normal position: In each dance the man and the lady mostly hold one another in a manner peculiar to that dance. The hold for the majority of the dance is referred to as the 'normal position'. Variants will occur from time to time and will be defined as required.

Open counter promenade position: Face your partner, then turn 45 degrees, the man to the right and the lady to the left. The man holds the lady's right hand in his left hand and the free arms are held to the side.

Open promenade position: Face your partner, then turn 45 degrees, the man to the left and the lady to the right. The man holds the lady's left hand in his right hand and the free arms are held to the side.

Outside partner: A forwards step usually on the right foot to your left of both your partner's feet. It may also be left foot forwards to your right of both your partner's feet.

Partner outside: A backwards step on either foot where your partner is stepping forwards 'outside partner' (see above).

Promenade position: From the close hold, the man turns his body to the left away from the lady. The lady turns her right side away from the man to form a V-shape. From the open hold, both the man and the lady turn outwards from each other – the man to the left and the lady to the right, forming a V-shape.

Rhythm break, rightwards or leftwards: A sideways group of steps using the basic rhythm of the dance but not closing feet neatly.

2/4 time: A musical term to indicate that there are two crotchets, or beats, in each bar of music.

Need to know more?

Choosing a dance studio

How do you select an appropriate school? Your main concern should be to ensure that your teacher has one of the three major qualification levels in one of the recognised teachers' organisations.

Under the heading 'Teachers' Organisations' you will see listed eight different bodies. The membership of each of these consists of dance teachers who have passed the appropriate examinations of the organisation. They are all members of, and are overseen by, a loosely knit body known as the British Dance Council, and all conform to common standards. If you contact them they will let you know their members in your area.

There are three levels of qualification. In ascending order they are: Associate (A), Licentiate (L) - sometimes called Member (M) - and Fellow (F), the highest level. The name of the association or society is often abbreviated to initials.

In respect of the dances in this book, teachers can have qualified in either a ballroom branch (BB) or a Latin branch (LA) of the appropriate body and this will sometimes be added to the qualification. For example, Lyndon Wainwright FIDTA (BB & LA) and Lynda King FIDTA (BB & LA) - Fellow of the International Dance Teachers' Association (Ballroom and Latin Branches).

Finally, many people are put off joining a school of dance by feelings of inadequacy or embarrassment. It is a great mistake. Dance teachers do realise this and you will be made welcome and made to feel comfortable irrespective of your previous experience.

UK dance organisations

Ballroom Dancers' Federation
12 Warren Lodge Drive
Kingswood
SURREY KT20 6QN
Tel/Fax: 01737 833737

Ballroom Dancers' Federation International
PO Box 2075 Kenley
SURREY CR8 5YP
Tel/Fax: 020 87631368

British Dance Council
Terpsichore House
240 Merton Road
South Wimbledon
LONDON SW19 1EQ
Tel: 020 8545 0085
Fax: 020 8545 0225

Central Council of Physical Recreation
Francis House, Francis Street
LONDON SW1P 1DE
Tel: 020 7854 8500
Fax: 020 7854 8501
www.ccpr.org.uk

Council for Dance Education and Training
Toynbee Hall
28 Commercial Street
LONDON E1 6LS
Tel: 020 7247 4030
Fax: 020 7247 3404
www.cdet.org.uk

World dance organisation

World Dance and Dance Sport Council
Karolinastrassa 20
28195 BREMEN
Germany
Tel: +49 421 13162
Fax: +49 421 14942

Teachers' organisations

Allied Dancing Association
137 Greenhill Road
LIVEROOL L18 7HQ
Tel: 0151 724 1829

British Association of Teachers of Dancing
23 Marywood Square
GLASGOW G41 2BP
Tel: 0141 423 4029
www.batd.co.uk

Imperial Society of Teachers of Dancing
22-26 Paul Street
LONDON EC2A 4QE
Tel: 020 7377 1577
Fax: 020 7247 8979
www.istd.org

International Dance Teachers' Association
76 Bennett Road
BRIGHTON BN2 5JL
Tel: 01273 685652
Fax: 01273 674388
www.idta.co.uk

National Association of Teachers of Dancing
44-47 The Broadway
THATCHAM
Berkshire RG19 3HP
Tel: 01635 868888
Fax: 01635 872301
www.natd.org.uk

Northern Counties Dance Teachers' Association
67 Elizabeth Drive
Palmersville
NEWCASTLE-UPON-TYNE
Tyne & Wear NE12 9QP
Tel: 0191 268 1830

Scottish Dance Teachers' Alliance
101 Park Road
GLASGOW G4 9JE
Tel: 0141 339 8944
Fax: 0141 357 4994

United Kingdom Alliance
Centenary House
38-40 Station Road
BLACKPOOL
Lancs FY4 1EU
Tel: 01253 408828
Fax: 01253 408066

Dance studios

England

Bedfordshire

Dance Fantasia
15 The Magpies
Bushmead
LUTON LU2 7XT
Tel: 01582-488529

Rayners School of Dancing
The Hall
Ashwell Avenue
Sundon Park
LUTON LU3 3AU
Tel: 01582 592510

Berkshire

Blanche Bateman Studio of Ballroom Dancing
23 Buckingham Avenue East
SLOUGH SL1 3EB
Tel/Fax 01753 520003

Spotlights Dance Centre
15 Marks Road
WOKINGHAM RG41 1NR
Tel: 0118 979 5044
www.spotlightsdance.com

Buckinghamshire

The Jill Foster Dance Centre
130 Wolverton Road
Stony Stratford
MILTON KEYNES MK11 1DN
Tel: 01908 563029

The Suzanne Lear School of Dancing
24 Sospel Court
FARNHAM ROYAL SL2 3BT
Tel: 01753 644612

Tracey's Dancezone
14 Cressey Avenue
Shenley Brook End
MILTON KEYNES MK5 7EL
Tel: 01908 504271

Cambridgeshire

Brown's Dance Studio
286 Lincoln Road
PETERBOROUGH PE3 9PJ
Tel: 01733 554282

DMJ Dancing
8 Othello Close
Hartford
HUNTINGDON PE29 1SU
Tel: 01480 458522/07803 184826

Maureen's School of Dancing
14 Augustus Way
CHATTERIS PE16 6DR
Tel: 01354 693218

Cheshire

Dance Fever
2 Ashfield House
Ashfield Road
SALE M33 7FE
Tel: 07973 921714
www.dancefever.uk.com

Lucy Diamond School of Dancing
Middlewich British Legion and Centura Club
MIDDLEWICH
Tel: 07929 051917

J. J. Foulds School of Dancing
Ashpoole House
LOWTON WA3 1BG
Tel: 01942 671270

Northwich Dance Company
c/o 16 Mayfair Drive
Kingsmead
NORTHWICH CW9 8GF
Tel: 01606 49050

Village Dancentre
9 Park Road Hale
ALTRINCHAM WA15 9NL
(Classes in Bowdon, Hazel Grove and Offerton)
Tel: 0161 928 9705

Cornwall

Tyler School of Dancing
'Topspin'
32 Trenance Avenue
NEWQUAY TR7 2HQ
Tel: 01637 873789

Derbyshire

Samantha-Jane Loades Academy of Dance
36a Frederick Avenue
ILKESTON DE7 4DW
Tel: 0115 932 3560/07946 389497

Devon

Chance to Dance
65 Churchill Road
EXMOUTH EX8 4DT
Tel: 01395 269782

Dance Latino
Renmark House 26 Elm Road
EXMOUTH EX8 2LG
Tel: 01395 277217

Lansdowne Dance Centre
16 Cadeell Park Road
TORQUAY TQ2 7JU
Tel: 01803 613580

Tanner-J Dance Zone
12 Redvers Grove
Plympton
PLYMOUTH PL7 1HU
Tel: 01752 283828

Westcountry Dance Studios
Inglenook Rockbeare Hill
EXETER EX5 2EZ
Tel: 01404 822942

Dorset

Bridport School of Dancing and Lyric Studios Stagecraft
9 Barrack Street
BRIDPORT DT6 3L4
Tel: 01308 427769

Dance Majic
Newtown Liberal Hall
316 Ringwood Road
Parkstone
POOLE
Tel: 01202 723381
www.dorsetdancecentre.co.uk

Durham

Lee Green Dance Centre
5 Lee Green
NEWTON AYCLIFFE DL5 5HN
Tel: 01325 318239

Richardson's Dance Studio
27–28 Fore Bondgate
BISHOP AUCKLAND DL14 7PE
Tel: 01388 609899
www.richardsonsdance studio.co.uk

Essex

Anderson Dance Group
226 Perry Street
BILLERICAY CM12 ONZ
Tel: 01277 633509
www.andersondancegroup.co.uk

A and M Dancing
5 St Mary's Road
BRAINTREE CM7 3JP
Tel: 01376 325753

Athene School of Dancing
Church Green
Broomfield
CHELMSFORD CM1 7BD
Tel: 0845 004 3062
www.pleisuredance.biz

King's Palais of Dance
WCA Market Road
WICKFORD SS12 0AG
Tel: 01375 375810

Spotlight DanceWorld
739a London Road
WESTCLIFF-ON-SEA SS0 9ST
Tel: 01702 474374

Steps Ahead School of Dancing
10 Griffith Close
Chadwell Heath
ROMFORD RM8 1TW
Tel: 07739 314596
www.stepsaheaddancing.com

Western Dance Centre
38 High Street
HADLEIGH SS9 2PB
Tel: 01702 559836
www.westerndancecentre.co.uk

Gloucestershire

Dancestars
37 Parry Road
GLOUCESTER GL1 4RZ
Tel: 01452 423 234

Foot Tappers School of Dancing
55 Dunster Close
TUFFLEY GL4 0TP
Tel: 01452 419324

Greater London

CK's Academy of Dance
16 St Marks Road
Bush Hill Park
ENFIELD EN1 1BE
Tel: 020 8482 4885
www.ckdance.co.uk

Dance Dayz
171 Henley Avenue
North Cheam
SUTTON SM3 9SD
Tel: 020 8641 5492

Dance Unlimited
74 Beresford Avenue
SURBITON KT5 9LW
Tel: 020 8339 8875
www.dance-unlimited.org

Hotsteps Dance Club
11b Station Road
ORPINGTON BR6 ORZ
Tel: 01689 822702
www.hotsteps.co.uk

Langley School of Dancing
Shepperton Village Hall
High Street
SHEPPERTON TW17 9AU
Tel: 020 8751 2177
www.langleydancing.co.uk

Pam's Dance Vogue
73 Hoylake Crescent
ICKENHAM UB10 8JQ
Tel: 01895 632143

Charles Richman
31 St Andrews Avenue
HORNCHURCH RM12 5DU
Tel: 07956 957038

Rita Sinclair
c/o 117 Burnway
HORNCHURCH RM11 3SW
Tel: 01708 471208/
07887 511468

Wedding and Emergency Dance Lessons
The Dance Matrix – Nationwide
Head Office: 115 Crofton Way
ENFIELD EN2 8HR
www.dancematrix.com

Wright Rhythm Dancing School
133 First Avenue
Bush Hill Park
ENFIELD EN1 1BP
Tel: 07801 414959

Yvonne's Dance School
12 Matlock Crescent
CHEAM SM3 9SP
www.dance-technique.co.uk

Hampshire

Angela's School of Dancing
Queens Road
ALDERSHOT GU11 3JE
Tel: 01252 332239

Basingstoke Dance Centre
25 Cavalier Road
Old Basing
BASINGSTOKE RG24 OEW
Tel: 01256 461665

Dance Connection of Gosport
Brune Park Community School
Military Road
GOSPORT PO12 3BJ
Tel: 01329 314061/
023 8046 6181
www.groups.msn.co.uk/
danceconnectionofgosport

Need to know more?

Diamond Dancentre
9 Queens Road
FARNBOROUGH GU14 6DJ
Tel: 01252 342118
www.diamonddancentre.
co.uk

Diment Macdonald Dance Centre
10 Spring Crescent
Portswood
SOUTHAMPTON SO17 2GA
Tel: 023 8055 4192
www.dimentmacdonald.co.uk

Fiesta Dance School
Trimdon
Poland
ODIHAM RG29 1JL
Tel: 01256 395110

Footsteps Dance School
73 Britten Road
Brighton Hill
BASINGSTOKE RG22 4HN
Tel: 01256 475619

Shuffles Dance Studio
Oak Farm Community
School
Chaucer Road
FARNBOROUGH
Tel: 01252 314291/
07774 151545
www.shuffles-dance.com

Spinners Dance Studio
4 Pardoe Close
Hedge End
SOUTHAMPTON SO30 0NE
Tel 01489 781513

Herefordshire

Allseasons School of Dance and Leisure
35 Friar Street
HEREFORD HR4 OAS
Tel:01432 353756
www.allseasonsdance.co.uk

Maureen's School of Dancing
41 Greengage Rise
Melbourn
ROYSTON SG8 6DS.
Tel: 01763 261680

Hertfordshire

Apton Dance Studio
Part Millers Two
The Maltings
BISHOPS STORTFORD
CM23 3DH
Tel: 01279 465381
www.aptondancestudio.com

The Dance Centre
1st Floor
24–26 High Street
HEMEL HEMPSTEAD HP1 3AE
Tel: 01442 252367

Kent

J. B.'s Dance Studio
90 St Michaels Street
FOLKESTONE CT20 1LS
Tel: 01303 252706

Hurcombe School of Dancing
34 Oxen Lease
Singleton
ASHFORD TN23 4YT
Tel: 01233 643411

Nicola Hyland School of Dancing
Sturry Social Centre
Sturry
NR. CANTERBURY
Tel: 07710 566827

Page/Mason School of Dancing
7 St Peter's Court
BROADSTAIRS CT10 2UU
Tel: 01843 863730

Rose School of Dancing
8 Bearsted Close
GILLINGHAM ME8 6LS
Tel: 01634 360105/235878

Lancashire

Haslingden Dance Centre
IDL Club George Street
Haslingden
ROSSENDALE
Tel: 01706 228693

Liberal School of Dancing
114 Burnley Road
Broadclough
BACUP OL13 8DB
Tel: 01706 872556

Northern Dance Connection
12 Holly Close
Clayton Le Woods
CHORLEY PR6 7JN
Tel: 01772 314551
www.dancefreeman.com

Leicestershire

118 Dance Studio
118 Charles Street
LEICESTER LE1 1LB
Tel: 0116 251 7073/289 2518

Premier Dancing Ltd
29–31 New Bond Street
LEICESTER LE1 4RQ
Tel: 0116 269 3618/251 1084
www.premierdance.co.uk

Lincolnshire

Cliftons Dance Academy
3 Turnberry Approach
Waltham
GRIMSBY DN37 OUQ
Tel: 01472 822270

Go Dance Studios
Tamer Court
Church Lane
SLEAFORD NG34 7DE
Tel: 01529 300930

Stevenson School of Dancing
Above 513 Grimsby Road
CLEETHORPES DN35 8AN
Tel: 01472 601069

London

A.C.W. Dance Studio
Office only:
Garden Flat
20a Melrose Road
SOUTHFIELDS SW18 1NE
Tel: 020 8871 0890
www.acwdancestudio.com

Central London Dance
13 Blandford Street
W1U 3DF
Tel: 020 7224 6004

Dancewise
1st Floor
370 Footscray Road
NEW ELTHAM SE9 2AA
Tel: 020 8294 1576
www.dancewise.co.uk

Flynn School of Dancing
40 Jago Close
PLUMSTEAD SE18 2TY
Tel: 01322 381070
Footsteps Stage School
(Chingford Loughton and Chigwell)
Tel: 020 8500 6943
www.footstepsdance school.com
Linda Fountain School of Dancing
6 Voss Court
STREATHAM SW16 3BS
Tel: 020 8679 3040
Dancemore
Robert Clack Centre
DAGENHAM RM8 1JU
Tel: 07761 209463
Bruce Smith Studio
Lacey Hall
Hazelwood Lane
PALMERS GREEN N13 6DE
Tel: 01920 468857/ 07702 188368

Greater Manchester

A Touch of Class
139 High Street
BOLTON BL3 1LX
Tel: 01204 861242
Danceland
55 Bridgewater Street
Little Hulton
WORSLEY M38 9ND
Tel: 0161 703 9577
Granada School of Dancing
St.Matthews Road
(above Conservative Club)
Edgeley
STOCKPORT SK3 9AM
Tel: 0161 480 6588
Parkfield Dance Centre
56 Eastwood Road
NEW MOSTON M40 3TF
Tel: 0161 682 4172
Sandham's Dance Studio
9a Peel Street
Farnworth
BOLTON BL4 8AA
Tel: 01204 795130
www.sandhams.co.uk

Village Dancentre
9 Park Road Hale
ALTRINCHAM WA15 9NL
Tel: 0161 928 9705

Merseyside

Debonaires at the Regency
84 Prescot Road
ST HELENS WA10 3TY
Tel: 01744 759466
www.debonairesatthe regency.com
The New Regency Dance Centre
c/o 35 Hill School Road
ST HELENS WA10 3BH
Tel: 01744 21061
Silhouette Dance Club
29 Hillbray Avenue
ST HELENS WA11 7DL
Tel: 01744 20136
www.silhouette-dance club.co.uk
Pat Thompson Dance Centre
110 Northway
Maghull
LIVERPOOL L31 1EF
Tel: 0151 526 1056/526 2010

Norfolk

Connaught Dance Centre
1 Laxton Close
ATTLEBOROUGH NR17 1QY
Tel: 01953 455500
Miller Dance and Performing Arts Centre
Units 1–3 Ropemakers Row
NORWICH NR3 2DG
Tel: 01603 488249
www.millerdance.co.uk
Tempo Schools of Dancing
55 Mallard Way
Bradwell
GREAT YARMOUTH NR31 8LX
Tel: 01493 665558

Northamptonshire

Margo's Dance Centre
204 Windmill Avenue
KETTERING NN15 7DG
Tel: 01536 312002

Tempo Dance Studio
Bath Road, Tailby House
KETTERING NN16 8NL
Tel: 01536 723656
www.tempodancestudio.co.uk

Nottinghamshire

Ann Culley School of Dance
26 Main Street
PAPPLEWICK NG15 8FD
Tel: 0115 963 3428/ 07711 946335
The L.A. School of Dance
13 Cheddar Close
Rainworth
MANSFIELD NG21 OHX
Tel: 01623 796431/ 07984 079568
Ray Needham School of Dance
9 Douglas Crescent
CARLTON NG4 1AN
Tel: 0115 841 1779/ 07973 939378
www.rayneedham.co.uk

Oxfordshire

Abingdon Dance Studios
59 Swinburne Road
ABINGDON OX14 2HF
Tel: 01235 520195
www.abingdondance.co.uk
Sarah Ayers School of Dance
20 Wytham View
Eynsham
OXFORD OX29 4LU
Tel: 01865 881208

Somerset

Davies School of Dance
12 The Hedges
St Georges
WESTON SUPER MARE
BS22 7SY
Tel: 01934 521338
www.davies-school-of-dance.co.uk
Langport Dance Centre
Bonds Farm
WEARNE (nr Langport)
TA10 OQQ
Tel: 01458 250322

Belinda Orford
Wayside Shepperdine Road
Oldbury Naite
BRISTOL BS35 1RJ
Tel: 01454 415346
PJ's Dance Academy
c/o 8 Meadow Drive
WESTON SUPER MARE
BS24 8BB
Tel: 01934 823948/
07855 827464

Staffordshire
Flair Dance Academy
60 Etchinghill Road
RUGELEY WS15 2LW
Tel: 01889 579558
Shaftesbury School of Dancing
48 Palmers Green
Hartshill
STOKE ON TRENT ST4 6AP
Tel: 01782 618180
www.shaftesburydance.com

Suffolk
Lait Dance Club
St Matthew's Hall
Clarkson Street
IPSWICH IP1 2JD
Tel: 01473 215543
www.laitdanceclub.co.uk
Miller Dance and Performing Arts Centre
58 Bridge Road
Oulton Road
LOWESTOFT NR32 3LR
Tel: 01502 573000
www.millerdance.co.uk

Sussex
Crawley Dance Academy
3 Tushmore Avenue
Northgate
CRAWLEY RH10 8LF
Tel: 01293 612538

Tyne & Wear
Newcastle Dance Centre
36–38 Grainger Park Road
NEWCASTLE-UPON-TYNE
NE4 8RY
Tel: 0191 273 9987
www.newcastledance
centre.co.uk

Warwickshire
DancinTime
Terpsichore Cottage
81 Alcester Road
STUDLEY B80 7NJ
Tel: 01527 852178
Jonstar School of Dancing
22 Gibson Crescent
BEDWORTH CV12 8RP
Tel: 024 7631 6592

West Midlands
Boscott's Dance Club
5 Long Wood
BOURNEVILLE B30 1HT
Tel: 0121 459 9167
Broadway Dance Centre
42 Livingstone Road
Perry Barr
BIRMINGHAM B20 3LL
Tel: 0121 356 4663
Inspire School of Dance
11 Alverley Road
Daimler Green
COVENTRY CV6 3LH
Tel: 024 7659 3359
Touch of Class Dancentre (incorporating The Midland Stage School of Performing Arts)
Holloway Hall
Court Passage, off Priory Street
DUDLEY DY1 3EX
Tel: 01384 235999/
07970 889251
www.freewebs.com/
touch-of-class-dancentre

Worcestershire
Catshill Dance Centre
Gibb Lane Catshill
BROMSGROVE B61 OJP
Tel: 01527 873638

Yorkshire East
Lacey School of Dancing
17 Grassdale Park
BROUGH HU15 1EB
Tel: 01482 666863
Lyndels Dancing Club
3 The Avenue
Melrose Street
HULL HU3 6EY
Tel: 01482 501248

Yorkshire North
Perry's Dancing
14 Haw Bank Court
SKIPTON BD23 1BY
Tel: 01756 794468 or 07900
285853
Playcraft Leisure School of Dancing
13 Kestrel Drive
Scotton
CATTERICK GARRISON DL9 3LX
Tel: 01748 830508

Yorkshire South
Joanne Armstrong School of Dancing
14 North End Drive
Harlington
DONCASTER DN5 7JS
Tel: 07979 758696
www.joannearmstrong.co.uk
Dentonia School of Dancing
Barnsley Road
Wombwell
BARNSLEY S73 8DJ
Tel: 01226 754684
Drapers Dance Centre
High Street
Beighton
SHEFFIELD S20 1ED
Tel: 0114 269 5703
Helen Neill School of Dance
41 Barnsley Road
Penistone
SHEFFIELD S36 8AD
Tel: 07771 610868

Yorkshire West

The D. M. Academy
The Studios
Briggate
SHIPLEY BD17 7BT
Tel: 01274 585317
www.dmacademy.co.uk

Horsforth Dance Academy
44 Hawksworth Avenue
GUISELEY
LEEDS LS20 8EJ
Tel: 01943 875894

Darren Peters Dance Centre
(Schools in Halifax, Thornton and Wilsden)
Tel: 07879 447106

Shandaw School of Dance
Serendipity Cottages
107-109 Gilstead Lane
Gilstead
BINGLEY BD16 3LH
Tel: 01274 510612
www.shandaw.co.uk

Wakefield Dance Group/ Wakefield City Slickers
82 Walton Lane
Sandal
WAKEFIELD WF2 6HQ
Tel: 01924 256624
www.members.lycos.co.uk/davidherries/index.htm

The Windsor School of Dancing
5 Willow Street
Girlington
BRADFORD BD8 9LT
Tel: 01274 488961
www.windsorballroom.co.uk

York Dance Studios
8 Radcliffe Road
Milnsbridge
HUDDERSFIELD HD3 4LX
Tel: 01484 643120
yorkdance.co.uk

Scotland

Johnny & Eleanor Banks
13 Paisley Avenue
EDINBURGH EH8 7LB
Tel: 0131 6613447

Ms N Clark
61 Balnagowan Drive
GLENROTHES
Fife KY6 2SJ
Tel: 01592 772685

John & Charlotte Comrie
76 Balmoral Avenue
Balmoral Gardens
Glenmavis
AIDRIE ML6 0PY

Andrew Cowan School of Dance
Community Central Hall
304 Maryhill Road
GLASGOW G20 7YE
Tel: 0141 6342129

Dees Dancing
PO Box 5456
GLASGOW G77 5LN
Tel: 0141 639 8300
www.deesdancing.co.uk

David Johnston
47 Polmont Road
Lauriestone
FALKIRK FK2 9QS
Tel: 01324 623007

Star Ballroom
10 Burnside Street
DUNDEE
Tel: 01382 611388

Christine Stevenson
(Various venues)
24 Ashgillhead Road
Larkhall
MOTHERWELL ML9 3AS
Tel: 01698 887296

Diane Swan Ballroom Dance Studio
72 Balnagask Road
ABERDEEN, AB11 8RE
Tel: 01224 876444

Warrens
(Various Glasgow venues)
Tel: 0141 942 7670

Wales

Dance Kingdom
Pharaoh House
Station Yard
New Dock Road
LLANELLI SA15 2EF
Tel: 01554 771543
dancekingdom.co.uk

Edwards Studio of Dance
Victoria House
Andrews Road
Llandaff North
CARDIFF CF14 2JP
Tel: 01222 575487 or 01222 843120

New Cottage Dance Centre
Ystrad-Mynach
HENGOED CF82 7ED
Tel: 01443 815909

Richards School of Dance
144 Rhys Stret
Trealaw
TONYPANDY CF40 2QF
Tel: 07929 079403

Index

Acknowledgements

Thanks to Mr B. Perry of Dancemore and Mr M. Kyberd of Michael's Dance Studio for providing the locations for the dance photography, and to the dancers:

Samba: Ben Petters and Jenna Fricker
Rumba: Joe Nichols and Natalie Hassan
Cha Cha Cha: Barry Perry and Chris Jaques
Salsa: Kyle Magee and Lisa Russell
Merengue: Keiran Smith and Theodora Karavasili
Disco/Freestyle: Keiran Smith and Shelly Tomlinson

Photo credits
Bananastock Ltd. pp. 2, 8, 72, 106, 136
Corbis pp. 43 (Bettmann/Corbis), 74 (Hulton-Deutsch Collection), 108 (Peter Williams)
Getty Images pp. 11, 18, 21, 166, 169
Ron Self p. 6
All other photographs by Christopher H. D. Davis

Collins need to know?

Look out for these recent titles in Collins' practical and accessible need to know? series.

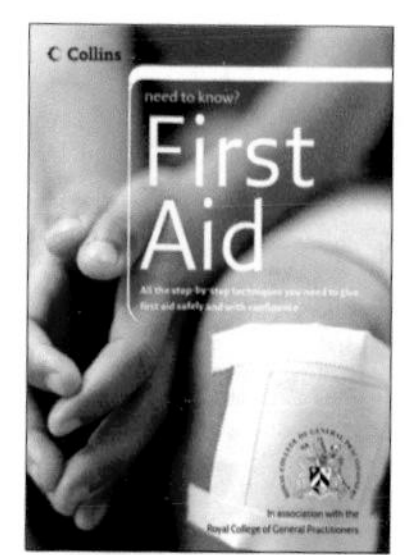

Other titles in the series:

Antique Marks
Birdwatching
Body Language
Buying Property in France
Buying Property in Spain
Card Games
Children's Parties
Codes & Ciphers
Decorating
Digital Photography
DIY
Dog Training
Drawing & Sketching
Dreams
Golf
Guitar
How to Lose Weight
Kama Sutra
Kings and Queens
Knots
Low GI/GL Diet
Pilates
Poker
Pregnancy
Property
Speak French
Speak Italian
Speak Spanish
Stargazing
Watercolour
Weddings
Wine
Woodworking
The World
Yoga
Zodiac Types

To order any of these titles, please telephone 0870 787 1732 quoting reference 263H.
For further information about all Collins books, visit our website: www.collins.co.uk